Barbara Willard

FIELD AND FOREST

Illustrated by Faith Jaques

KESTREL BOOKS

KESTREL BOOKS
Published by Penguin Books Ltd
Harmondsworth, Middlesex, England

First published in 1975

ISBN 0 7226 5856 7

Printed in Great Britain
by Ebenezer Baylis & Son, Limited
The Trinity Press, Worcester, and London

Contents

The Seasons

The Hunt

People

Enchantment

Acknowledgements

The publishers and editor would like to thank the following for permission to use copyright material: for 'Suffolk Ploughmen' from *Akenfield: Portrait of an English Village* by Ronald Blythe to David Higham Associates and Allen Lane; for 'Babes in the Wood' and 'Sheep-Shearing Song' from *A Song for Every Season* by Bob Copper to William Heinemann Ltd and Coppersongs; for 'Advice' and 'The Rain' from *The Complete Poems of W. H. Davies* to Mrs H. M. Davies and Jonathan Cape Ltd; for 'Logs', 'Snow', 'The Pigs and the Charcoal Burner', 'The Scarecrow', 'The Ride-by-Nights', 'The Ghost Chase' and 'In the Forest' from *The Complete Poems of Walter de la Mare* to the Literary Trustees of Walter de la Mare, and the Society of Authors as their representative; for 'Anthony Crundle' from *Olton Pools* by John Drinkwater to Sidgwick & Jackson Ltd; for extract from *The Golden Bough* by Sir James G. Frazer to the Estate of Sir James G. Frazer and A. P. Watt & Son; for 'Pan With Us' from *The Poetry of Robert Frost* edited by Edward Connery Lathem to the Estate of Robert Frost, Jonathan Cape Ltd and Holt, Rinehart & Winston Inc.; for extract from *Lady into Fox* by David Garnett to Chatto & Windus Ltd; for 'The Good Spirit of Sherwood' from *The Adventures of Robin Hood* by Roger Lancelyn Green to Penguin Books Ltd; for 'The Year's Awakening' from *Collected Poems* by Thomas Hardy to the Trustees of the Hardy Estate, Macmillan of London and Basingstoke and the Macmillan Company of Canada Ltd; for 'November' from *Gloucestershire* by F. W. Harvey to P. W. H. Harvey; for 'Blackberry Picking' from *Death of a Naturalist* by Seamus Heaney to Faber & Faber Ltd; for 'Harvest Customs' from *English Custom and Usage* by Christina Hole to B. T. Batsford Ltd; for 'A Shropshire Lad' from *Collected Poems* by A. E. Housman to The Society of Authors as the literary representative of the Estate of A. E. Housman and Jonathan Cape Ltd; for 'Hawk Roosting' from *Lupercal* by Ted Hughes to Faber & Faber Ltd; for 'The Way through the Woods' from *Rewards and Fairies* by Rudyard Kipling to Mrs George Bambridge, Macmillan of London and Basingstoke, Macmillan Company of Canada and A. P. Watt & Son; for 'First Sight' from *The Whitsun Weddings* by Philip Larkin to Faber & Faber Ltd; for 'Nottingham and the Mining Country' from *Phoenix* by D. H. Lawrence to Laurence Pollinger Ltd and the Estate of the late Mrs Frieda Lawrence; for 'The Knight's Story' from *Undine* by Mary Macgregor to Thomas Nelson & Sons Ltd; for 'The Waggon-Maker' and 'The Ghost Heath Run' from *Reynard the Fox* by John Masefield to the Society of Authors as the literary representative of the Estate of John Masefield and the Macmillan Publishing Co.; for 'The Dapple-Grey Palfrey' from *Aucassin and Nicolette and Other Tales* translated by Pauline Matarasso to Penguin Books Ltd; for 'Hop-Picking' from *Collected*

Essays, Journalism & Letters Volume 1 by George Orwell to Mrs Sonia Brownell Orwell and Secker & Warburg Ltd; for 'Forest Brotherhood' from *Dr Zhivago* by Boris Pasternak to William Collins Sons & Co. Ltd; for 'Trees in the Moonlight' from *Blackbird in the Lilac* by James Reeves to Oxford University Press; for 'The Red Scourge of the Forest' from *Red Fox* by Sir Charles G. D. Roberts to Kestrel Books and McGraw-Hill Ryerson Ltd; for 'A Medieval Hunt' from *Sir Gawain and the Green Knight* translated by Brian Stone to Penguin Books; for 'The Hollow Wood' from *Collected Poems* by Edward Thomas to Myfanwy Thomas and Faber & Faber Ltd; for 'May Day' from *Lark Rise to Candleford* by Flora Thompson to Oxford University Press; for 'The Old Forest' from *The Lord of the Rings* by J. R. R. Tolkien to George Allen & Unwin Ltd; for extract from *The Forest People* by Colin Turnbull to Jonathan Cape Ltd and Simon & Schuster Inc.; for 'The Harvest' from *The Country Child* by Alison Uttley to Faber & Faber Ltd; for 'A Witches' Sabbath in the English Countryside' from *Lolly Willowes* by Sylvia Townsend Warner to Chatto & Windus Ltd; for extract from *Tarka the Otter* by Henry Williamson to The Bodley Head; for 'The Poacher' from *Capreol: The Story of a Roebuck* by Richard Williamson to Macdonald Ltd; for 'The Hawk' from *The Collected Poems of W. B. Yeats* to M. B. Yeats, Miss Anne Yeats, Macmillan of London and Basingstoke, Macmillan Company of Canada and A. P. Watt and Son; for 'The Last Snow' from *Complete Poems of Andrew Young* edited by Leonard Clark to Secker & Warburg Ltd.

Preface

Once upon a time, on the edge of a deep dark forest . . . Scores
of fairy tales open with those words. However often one
reads them, the feeling remains – of mystery and stillness, of
unknown powers working in the shadows. Witches, woodcutters, wolves – all have their place in such wild parts. Even
today, when forests are mostly tamed, it is possible to stand
within a merely sizeable wood and feel strangely threatened.
Perhaps it is the knowledge, barely admitted, that however
cunningly man may have worked over the centuries to make
the world his own, the trees were there long ages before he
thought of clearing them away to let in the light and make
stretches of pasture and arable. The inherited wisdom of
those ages seems still to be carried in every leaf and twig.
It is rather as if they know their power. Man needs only to
relax his guard and turn away, and the trees take over again.
Even in climates where growth is slow, fields that have been
grazed or ploughed do not take so very long to vanish under
scrub and saplings.

In the days of which the best stories are told, every prince,
knight or poor man's son setting out to seek his fortune was
bound to brave the dangers of the forest. It covered such
great stretches of the world that villages, even cities, were
like islands in its immensity. It was a testing ground for
heroes, who, as we know, encountered many hazards there,
fell victim to many enchantments and terrors before emerging
at last into the sunlight and success of an accomplished
mission. Disguised as woodcutters or humble esquires,
princes ride boldly down the dark and silent glades to rescue
ladies bewitched into the shape of mouse or hare. Lovers
flee to the forest to escape the tyranny of overbearing parents.
Disinherited younger sons, supporters of lost causes, leaders
fleeing from political persecution have always found refuge in
the forest. It is the home of outlaws, of sorcerers. All such
flourish *under the greenwood tree*; and at least one genuine
fugitive monarch of our own owed his life to an oak tree's
fine concealing foliage.

The home of many wild things, the forest must be a
hunting ground. In fact this is how the word *forest* is most

often defined – not always as a place of trees, but as *a tract kept waste for hunting*; as an *unenclosed woodland district owned by the sovereign and kept for hunting; an unenclosed royal hunting ground*. All are dictionary definitions and they present an image romantic and exciting. King and nobles ride to the hunt; in deep glades the deer lift startled heads and stand poised for flight; the horn sounds. Riders and hounds stream through copse and spinney and up over great tracts of heath, weaving in and out of sunlight, shouting, hallooing . . . And in some distant place at the end of the long run, the stag turns at bay, the hounds leap and tear, the sport ends triumphantly amid blood and congratulation. Then home to great haunches of venison, deep draughts of wine in some high hall filled with smoke and minstrelsy . . .

A forest is *trees and undergrowth sometimes mixed with pasture* says yet another dictionary. It is possible at times to stand on high ground above a farm surrounded by forest, either trees or heath, and see how such places were won from the wild by smaller men than those bent on raising cities and kingdoms. A dwelling was first built above a stream, perhaps, and the land seized and cleared, bit by laborious bit, until all the ground between that stream and the next one conveniently flowing had become fertile farmland. This happened with ever-growing speed as populations grew bigger, as wood became increasingly a vital commodity. Not only was man cradled and coffined in wood, supping his broth with a wooden spoon from a wooden bowl, cooking and warming himself at a wood fire in a timber-framed dwelling – he also needed wood for industrial fuel, for burning into charcoal to feed the furnaces and forges of a time when iron was used more and more for armaments as well as for ploughs and horseshoes. For *guns and gunstones*, as they said. In the southern parts of England in the sixteenth century they found themselves threatened with a severe shortage of timber. There was an almost panic reaction to this situation, with petitions to parliament, prayers to the sovereign, to check what seemed the immoderate and fatal use of so much wood for charcoal. For how should they build ships and houses, how repair barns and farms if all the trees were hewn down?

11

Life has always been hard for the worker on the land, whether in forest or field; but perhaps hardest of all for the *poor woodcutter* of the romances, struggling to maintain himself and his family. He was greatly oppressed by bitterly harsh laws against poaching venison and game, property of the King, who killed for sport what the peasant needed for subsistence. Yet out of all this roughness and toughness, as the forest is thrust back, comes the sylvan and the pastoral vision, the delight of poets, the repository of unnumbered traditions of sowing and harvest. Though Shakespeare wrote bleakly of the winter round, when *icicles hang by the wall*, when *milk comes frozen home in pail*, he wrote blithely of the reverse image – the early summer time; for then *daisies pied and violets blue . . . Do paint the meadows with delight . . .* Field and forest have inspired writers of all kinds for hundreds and hundreds of years. There is enough poetry alone about wild things in wild places, about the seasonal round of the farmer and his boy, to fill a score of libraries. There are numberless stories, romantic, adventurous, set against a background of tree and bush, haunted by birds and animals, telling of man's strange affinity with the element out of which he came.

We still have the remnants of our ancient forests, and they are reputedly protected from encroachment by old laws often reinforced by newer ones. But covetous eyes are cast on what remains, since we live in a land-hungry age and already have too little space to house all our people. If those ancient laws are ever relaxed, then the acres covered with heather and gorse, birch and beech, oak and spruce must vanish under the harsh ugliness of a vast urban sprawl.

Then the last vestiges of the primitive forests that once spread over all the land would be buried until another age came to cover the ashes of our own. Then deer and fox, otter and badger, coney and squirrel would find no refuge. No nesting place, no feeding ground would exist for our great companies of birds. From wren and goldcrest to heron and swan these creatures would vanish as completely as the wild boar that was hunted in the days of the Tudors right to the outskirts of London . . .

LIVING THINGS

Advice

Now, you two eyes, that have all night been sleeping,
Come into the meadows, where the lambs are leaping;
See how they start at every swallow's shadow
That darts across their faces and their meadow.
See how the blades spring upright, when the Sun
Takes off the weight of raindrops, one by one.
See how a shower, that freshened leaves of grass,
Can make the bird's voice fresher than it was.
See how the squirrels lash the quiet trees
Into a tempest, where there is no breeze!
Now, you two eyes, that have all night been sleeping,
Come into the meadows, where the lambs are leaping.

W. H. DAVIES

A Walk in the Forest

I love the Forest and its airy bounds,
Where friendly Campbell* takes his daily rounds;
I love the breakneck hills, that headlong go,
And leave me high, and half the world below;
I love to see the Beech Hill mounting high,
The brook without a bridge, and nearly dry.
There's Buckhurst Hill, a place of furze and clouds,
Which evening in a golden haze enshrouds;
I hear the cows go home with tinkling bell,
And see the woodman in the forest dwell,
Whose dog runs eager where the rabbit's gone;
He eats the grass, then kicks and hurries on;
Then scrapes for hoarded bone, and tries to play,
And barks at larger dogs and runs away.

JOHN CLARE

* The gamekeeper.

15

The Golden Bough

J. G. FRAZER

In the religious history of the Aryan race in Europe the worship of trees has played an important part. Nothing could be more natural. For at the dawn of history Europe was covered with immense primeval forests, in which the scattered clearings must have appeared like islets in an ocean of green. Down to the first century before our era the Hercynian forest stretched eastward from the Rhine for a distance at once vast and unknown; Germans whom Caesar questioned had travelled for two months through it without reaching the end. Four centuries later it was visited by the Emperor Julian, and the solitude, the gloom, the silence of the forest appear to have made a deep impression on his sensitive nature. He declared that he knew nothing like it in the Roman empire. In our own country the wealds of Kent, Surrey and Sussex are remnants of the great forest of Anderida, which' once clothed the whole of the south-eastern portion of the island. Westward it seems to have stretched till it joined another forest that extended from Hampshire to Devon. In the reign of Henry II the citizens of London still hunted the wild bull and boar in the woods of Hampstead. Even under the later Plantagenets the royal forests were sixty-eight in number. In the forest of Arden it was said that down to modern times a squirrel might leap from tree to tree for nearly the whole length of Warwickshire . . .

(from *The Golden Bough*, 1890–1915)

Logs

This tree by April wreathed in flowers
That sheened with leaves the summer hours,
   In dappling shine and shade,
Now all that then was lovely lacks,
Is vanquished by the saw and axe,
   And into firewood made.

How happy and gentle a daybreak song
Whispered its solemn boughs among,
   At sigh of morning stirred;
It braved the dangerous lightning; rose
In splendour, crowned with winter's snows;
   And sheltered every bird
That perched with slender claw and wing
To preen, to rest, to roost, to sing,
   Unseen – but not unheard.

But came the Woodman with his axe
   Into the sun-sweet glade;
And what was once all beauty and grace
   Is into firewood made.

WALTER DE LA MARE

The Dapple-Grey Palfrey

Translated from the French by Pauline Matarasso

Here is a tale set and indeed written in chivalric times, a tale of love and cunning, in which the encircling forest is ever present, and which, in fact, supplies the final solution to the lovers' problems. The story comes to us in a spanking translation from the Medieval French. In spite of this, it is sometimes a shade long-winded, so here it has been speeded up every now and again . . .

*

Now the story relates that in the county of Champagne there lived a most valorous and courtly knight, whose heart was high but whose funds were low, as you will have occasion to discover. It is meet that I should describe his merits and the valour that animated him, since in many and sundry quarters he was held in high regard as a man of judgement, honour and distinction, stout-hearted in the extreme. Had he been as loaded with wealth as he was fired with excellence (saving he grew the worse for having it), he would have been without peer or fellow . . . At tournaments, when his head was iron-clad, he had no time for dallying with the ladies outside the barricades; there where the press was thickest he would hurl himself full tilt; no novice he, when he was armed and mounted. There was never a day in the depths of winter when he did not sport a gay gown, which could be seen to reflect his sunny disposition. His good cheer was the more admirable in that his holding was of little value: his lands did not bring him in above two hundred pounds a year, and so it was that he travelled far and wide in search of renown.

The knight was much taken up at this time with an honest and noble passion for a high-born maiden, the daughter of a worthy prince, a man of might and substance; far from being

18

in want, he had an abundance of goods and chattels, and his coffers were well filled. His lands were worth at least a thousand pounds a year to him, and he had many requests for the hand of his charming daughter whose great beauty was a lure to all and sundry. This prince was a widower in the decline of life who had no other children; his castle stood amid deep woods, encircled by a wide expanse of forest. The other knight in my story aspired to the hand of this knight's daughter, but her father opposed his suit, neither wanting him to love her nor her to be gossiped about on his account. The young knight went by the name of Sir William, and he too lived in the forest where the rich old lord dwelled, well entrenched in his vast lands and great possessions. The manors were two leagues apart, but there was no keeping love within their confines, for the two young people did not dissipate their mental energies on extraneous matters. When the knight wished to meet with his beloved, because of idle talk about him and her he took a path he had made through the dense sweep of the forest . . . But the difficulties were great: he could not speak to her at close quarters as he longed to do, for the courtyard was stoutly fenced and walled. The maiden dared not pass the gate, but she had such solace as was afforded her by speaking to him frequently through the planking of a palisade. A deep ditch on the outside and a dense bank of thorn bushes prevented their drawing close. The castle stood on a rock; it was strongly fortified and had a drawbridge as the entrance. As for the old knight, who had guile enough for any contingency and whose life was nearly spent, he rarely left the house, being past riding, but stayed at home in peace. He had his daughter closely watched, and she often sat with him to entertain him, which was not to her taste, for she was deprived of the pleasure on which her heart was set. Sir William meanwhile, who was a man of sense, did not let the grass grow under his feet; when he saw there was no alternative he gave up asking for permission to see her, but regularly visited her abode, although he could not cross the threshold. He did not see the lovely prisoner at nearly such close range as his heart desired, and for all his frequent visits he had little to feast his eyes on, for there was no place that she could reach which afforded him a full view of her face, and both the lovers declared that their hearts were breaking.

The knight, who could not but adore a maiden whose perfections set her far above all others, had, so the story affirms, a magnificent palfrey of the most brilliant dapple grey. It would be impossible to pick out any flower that could compare with it for beauty of form or hue, nor was there a kingdom at that time which could boast so fine a creature or so quiet and comfortable a ride. The knight thought the world of it and, I tell you truly, would not have parted with it for a fortune. Over a long period it was seen in his possession by the people of the locality. He would often set off on this palfrey to woo the maiden, riding through the lonely deeps of the forest where he had trodden the track unknown to any save himself and his horse . . .

(At last, frustration forced Sir William to action. He bearded his beloved's father in his castle, put forward his suit – and was sent smartly packing. Gloomily he told the lady what had happened . . .)

'The old and the young, it seems to me, *(said the maid)* have very different ambitions. However, if you do as I would have you, you cannot fail to win me . . .'

'Upon my faith, sweet maid, that will I, without fail,' replied the knight. 'Just tell me what you want.'

'I have been thinking,' said she, 'of something which has been in my mind for a long time. You know, of course, that you have an uncle who is very rich; he holds sway over a vast domain, and in wealth and might he is my father's equal. He has neither child, wife, nor brother, nor any closer kin than you, and it is known for a fact that on his death it will all be yours. His treasure and rents are worth more than sixty gold marks. Go over now to see him without a moment's delay. He is old and failing as you know; explain to him that . . . if he would promise you land enough to bring you three hundred pounds in rent, and were to come in person to . . . my father who holds him in affection . . . and to say . . . : "My nephew will receive a portion of my domain with a rentable value of three hundred pounds against your daughter's hand: it will be a good match," then I am sure he would consent to it . . . And having married me, you would then hand back to your uncle the land he had promised you. I am so wholly committed to your love that I should be only too happy with the bargain.'

'Believe me, fair maid,' replied the knight, 'I never wanted anything as much. I will put it to my uncle right away.'

He took his leave and rode off the way he had come, plunged in the black and gloomy thoughts begotten by the refusal he had met with. As he rode through the forest astride his dapple-grey palfrey the dismay he felt was none the less much lightened by the prudent and honest counsel that the maiden had given him. He rode without let or hindrance straight to Medet where his uncle lived . . .

(The uncle seemed very friendly and ready to help. While

21

Sir William rode off to a tournament some miles away – where he intended to acquit himself gloriously and thus increase his chances as a suitor – the old uncle hurried off to consult with that other old man, the girl's father. And then – treachery! The uncle presented himself as a suitor for his nephew's beloved. What's more, he was rapturously accepted by the maid's avaricious father, who cared nothing for his daughter's happiness, being interested entirely in material gain. . . .)

'Alas, unhappy wretch that I am, (*the lady cried*) this is the end of me! What a shameful trick that old man played! Death would be too good for him! How vilely he has deceived his nephew, such a good and noble knight and rich in every virtue. Now, thanks to his wealth and might, I am already bestowed on that old greybeard. May God give him his just deserts! He has meddled in pure madness, for I shall never know a day's happiness again and he will have got himself a mortal enemy the day he marries me.'

After some parleying it was settled that the maiden should be married at daybreak, and orders were given for her to be attired by her maids-in-waiting who, on considering the day and hour appointed, were most put out and pulled long faces at the news. The father asked those to whom the instructions had been given if his daughter was ready, and if she was at all nervous, and whether anything was lacking that she ought to have.

'Nothing, good sir, that we know of,' answered one of her maidens, 'provided we have enough palfreys and saddles to take us all to the church, for I expect there will be a great crowd of kinswomen and cousins who live in the vicinity.'

'We are not unduly worried about palfreys,' he replied, 'I think we shall have enough. There is not a baron in the neighbourhood who has not been asked to send one.'

The squire to whom this mission had been entrusted lost no time in going to the house of that knight who was a very repository of valour and a shining light of prowess. The sage and noble William little thought that the marriage negotiations had reached such a stage, but the tug of love at his heartstrings had brought him hurrying home. He could think of nothing but the matter that obsessed him: love blossomed in his heart. He had returned from the tournament in a far from dismal mood, for he fully expected to wed the maiden who had so recently been refused him as soon as God willed and the occasion offered. Each day he waited on the coming of glad tidings, expecting his uncle to send him word to go and wed his wife. He sang as he went about the house, and had a minstrel play a new air on his viol; having won outright the prize of the tournament he was in the best and blithest of spirits. His glance was forever straying towards the gate to see whether anyone was bringing him news . . .

But now of a sudden a squire came riding into the courtyard. When Sir William caught sight of him his heart leaped in his breast, a-flutter with joy.

'God save you, sir,' said the messenger. 'I have been sent here on an errand by the ancient who is, as you know, your friend of long standing. You have a priceless palfrey, there's not a horse in the world with smoother paces: my lord sends you a pressing request to lend it him for friendship's sake, so that he may have it by tonight.'

'For what purpose, friend?'

'Sir, to take his daughter, our lovely and charming young mistress, to the church.'

'And wherefore will she be going?'

'Why, good sir, to wed your uncle, to whom she has been given. Tomorrow at daybreak my mistress is to be taken up to the lonely chapel at the far end of the forest. Make haste, sir, I stay too long; lend your uncle and my lord your palfrey – the best there is in the kingdom, that I know: it's been put to the proof time and again.'

Sir William, on hearing this, exclaimed:

'God! is it true I've been betrayed by my uncle in whom I put my trust and whom I entreated so civilly to help me in my enterprise? May the Almighty never forgive him his treachery and crime! I can scarcely credit his doing such a thing; I don't believe you are telling the truth.'

'You will be able to verify it tomorrow before the hour of prime is rung; there's already a great gathering of the old knights of the country.'

23

'Alas!' cried the other, 'how vilely I have been betrayed and tricked!'

He was on the point of collapsing in a faint from shock and grief and was only saved by his fear of incurring the poor opinion of his household; he was so stricken and incensed that he did not know what to do or say. He abandoned himself to his grief, and while he was in this state of agitation the messenger continued to press his suit:

'Sir, have your good palfrey saddled quickly, and seeing it is so smooth a ride it can carry my mistress up to the church.'

(*At first the knight was furiou sat the idea of lending his own beautiful dapple-grey palfrey to carry to church the girl he had hoped to wed there himself. Then he decided that she was so sweet and good and lovely that he would pay her this last tribute. So the squire led the palfrey back to his master's castle, where the wedding guests, a huge collection of the most ancient knights and noblemen from all the countryside around, were making merry on the wedding eve. At dawn the watchman, as befuddled with drink and merrymaking as all the rest, summoned them from brief slumber . . .*)

'Arise, my lords, the dawn is breaking!' he cried, all fuddled with the wine he had drunk that evening. The household, who had rested little and slept less, stumbled dazedly to their feet; the squires made haste to saddle up, thinking dawn would soon be upon them: but before the peep of day they would have time to cover five good leagues at an easy pace. The palfreys were saddled, and all the aged knights who were to accompany the maid to her marriage service in the old chapel at the farthest end of the deep and desolate forest had mounted, and the girl was entrusted to the sagest of them all. The saddle was set on the dapple-grey palfrey, and when it was led up the maiden's grief broke out more violently than before. The old men in their wisdom were quite oblivious of what was going on in her mind, but imagined that she was weeping at leaving her father's house for a strange hearth: the cause of her tears and unbridled grief escaped them utterly. It was with great difficulty that she was mounted at all.

24

They all set out in a group and headed, as I remember, straight for the forest; they found the path too narrow to permit their riding two abreast and those who formed the maiden's escort fell to the rear while the rest went on ahead. The knight who rode on her right hand, seeing the way so strait, placed her in front while he fell in behind her, as the narrowness of the track commanded. The road was interminably long and they were tired and jaded from lack of sleep, in fact they were just about worn out . . . Over hill and dale they rode, nodding on their horses' necks . . . Most of them were slumped in the saddle; a few were awake, their thoughts anywhere but on the business of escorting the maiden. On and on they jogged on their weary way through the deep forest, with the maiden, in her anguish, wishing she were in London or in Winchester.

The dapple-grey palfrey was well acquainted with this

narrow, disused track, having plodded along it on many occasions. They picked their way down a steep incline where the forest was so dense that the moonlight hardly penetrated it: the shade of the close woodland was particularly thick down in the deep-sunk valley bottom . . . Now as I understand it, the grey palfrey, which the maiden was riding in the wake of the main body, was not familiar with the farther reaches of the track that the rest of the party was now entering on, but spied a little path to the right which led straight towards Sir William's habitation. At the sight of this path, which it had often followed, it left the main track and the bevy of horses without a moment's hesitation. The knight who was detailed to escort the maiden had fallen so deeply asleep that from time to time his palfrey stopped by the way, and the maiden was left with none to convey her but God. She loosed the reins and gave the palfrey its head, and it set off down the overgrown path. Not one of the knights noticed that the maiden was no longer following them, and before they became aware of the fact they had covered a league and more . . .

The palfrey followed the path without straying to left or right, for it had trodden it many a time, winter and summer. The unhappy maiden, having started down it, kept looking around her for the knights and barons, but in vain; the forest was deep and dark and hazardous and she was dismayed at finding herself alone . . . She commended herself to God's keeping, and the dapple-grey palfrey carried her on. Dejected and anxious, she gave her mount its head, and never uttered a sound for fear the others should hear her and come back for her; to die in the woods was preferable to contracting such a marriage. Such were her thoughts as she rode along, and the palfrey, keen to get home by the familiar route, covered so much ground at its easy amble that it swiftly reached the perimeter of that great tract of woodland. At the foot of a slope a river flowed swift and dark. The grey palfrey, which knew the ford, headed straight towards it and lost no time in crossing over. They had not left its narrow shallows far behind, when, from the quarter the palfrey was making for, the maiden heard the sound of a horn. Above the main gate stood the watchman, heralding the dawn with trumpet blast.

The maiden rode straight towards the sound till she found herself beneath the castle, bewildered and distraught, like some errant soul who has lost his way and doesn't know how to ask it. The palfrey however, never faltering in its course, stepped on to the drawbridge which spanned a deep moat running right round the castle. The watchman blowing his horn above heard the clip-clop of the palfrey's hoofs on the bridge it had so often crossed. He stopped winding his horn and was silent for a while: then he climbed down from his look-out and called out sharply:

'Who comes riding so hard across the bridge at this hour?'

'Assuredly the most unhappy girl ever born of woman,' came the answer. 'For God's sake let me come in until I see the dawn break, for I don't know where to go.'

'Damsel,' replied the other, 'you can take it for certain that I wouldn't dare to let you or anyone else enter this castle without my lord's leave. There was never a man in such distress as he is: his spirits are quite crushed, so cruelly has he been abused.'

While he was speaking of this he brought his eyes level with a judas in the postern gate. There was no need of a candle or lantern, for the moon was shining brightly. He saw the dapple-grey palfrey and recognized it all right, though he looked at it carefully first, much puzzled as to how it had got there. The maiden too, who was holding the reins, came under close scrutiny, in her rich attire and new, resplendent clothes. Then he scurried off to see his lord who was lying in bed in cheerless solitude.

'Sir,' he said, 'your pardon, but there's a woman all for-lorn – young by her looks and splendidly apparelled, who has come out of the woods. Her garb is sumptuous: I think she is wearing a rich, furred cape, and her gown appears to be of the finest cloth. The young lady, who looks sad and woebegone, is seated on your dapple-grey palfrey. Her speech does her no injustice, on the contrary she is so pretty and gracious that, without exaggeration, sir, I don't believe there's another maid in the country to compare with

27

her. If you ask me, she's a fairy sent here by God to compensate you for the injury which is weighing so heavily on your spirits. You have got fair value for the maiden you have lost.'

On hearing this Sir William sprang to his feet without waiting for more. Covered only with a surcoat he came running to the gate and had it quickly opened. The maid called out to him in plaintive tones:

'Ah! noble knight, I have endured so much fatigue this night! For the love of God, sir, if it's no trouble to you, let me into your manor: I have no wish to tarry long, but I go in mortal fear of being pursued by certain knights who are very much alarmed at having lost me. I have come to ask your protection, chance having brought me here, for I have lost my way and am in dire distress.'

Sir William was overcome with joy at hearing her. He recognized the palfrey that had been so long in his stable, and he recognized the maiden, too, on sight, and I tell you truly that no happier man could possibly exist. He led her inside and lifted her down from her horse, and taking her right hand in his he kissed her more than twenty times, at which she made not the least demur, for she had recognized him too. The two of them were so delighted at seeing one another that they forgot all their woes. She was helped off with her cape, and they both sat down on a quilt of richest silk, edged with gold, and crossed themselves at least twenty times apiece, for they could hardly believe they were not dreaming. When there were no servants around they were not at a loss to solace themselves with kisses, but I assure you that no other impropriety took place on that occasion. The maiden recounted her adventure from beginning to end and swore that she must have been born under a lucky star for God to have brought her thither and delivered her, with only chance to guide her, from the clutches of her aged suitor, who was expecting a good return on his outlay of goods and money. When morning lightened Sir William went to attire himself. He had the maiden brought to his chapel within the walls and, sending for his chaplain on the spot, he got himself married without recall and joined in valid matrimony, whose bonds are not easily put asunder.

And when mass had been sung, servants, waiting-maids and squires roistered and celebrated in the palace.

This outcome, though, was bound to be most unpalatable to those who had lost the maiden through their folly. They had arrived in a body at the lonely chapel, each and every one in a state of exhaustion and distress from the night-long ride. The ancient asked for his daughter, and the knight who had taken such poor care of her did not know what to say . . . In the midst of this turmoil his companions sighted a squire coming up the track at the gallop; he rode straight up to the ancient and announced:

'My lord, Sir William assures you of his warm friendship. He married your daughter this very morning at dawn, to his great happiness and joy. You are to come over right away, my lord, and he invites his uncle, too, who played him false; he forgives him this injury now that your daughter is bestowed on him . . .'

Thus, my lords, did it please God that this marriage, which found favour in His sight, be lastingly established. Sir William was a sterling knight, as courtly as he was valorous; he never abandoned his pursuit of chivalry, but strove even harder for renown, winning the friendship of counts and princes. Within three years, according to the tale, the ancient died, leaving Sir William all he had. So the latter found himself holding lands worth a good thousand pounds a year, and administered justice throughout the great and well-defended domain. Death claimed his powerful uncle next, and William, who was no simpleton, nor of a mean or craven nature, nor given to speaking ill of his neighbours, added his uncle's lands to his, unchallenged by any. And so this tale that I have rhymed I now conclude in accordance with the true facts of the story.

(from *Aucassin and Nicolette and Other Tales*, 1971)

Binsey Poplars

felled 1879

My aspens dear, whose airy cages quelled,
Quelled or quenched in leaves the leaping sun,
All felled, felled, are all felled;
   Of a fresh and following folded rank
      Not spared, not one
      That dandled a sandalled
     Shadow that swam or sank
On meadow and river and wind-wandering weed-winding
  bank.

O if we but knew what we do
     When we delve or hew –
  Hack and rack the growing green!
     Since country is so tender
  To touch, her being só slender,
  That, like this sleek and seeing ball
  But a prick will make no eye at all,
  Where we, even where we mean

     To mend her we end her,
    When we hew or delve:
After-comers cannot guess the beauty been.
  Ten or twelve, only ten or twelve
    Strokes of havoc únselve
     The sweet especial scene,
    Rural scene, a rural scene,
    Sweet especial rural scene.

GERARD MANLEY HOPKINS

The Sounding of the Call

JACK LONDON

Half dog, half wolf, Buck works among the snowy northlands, the Canada of gold-rush days. He is deeply devoted to his master, John Thornton, who has rescued him from a life of brutality. But the wolf strain in Buck proves stronger than his love for his master. When the ancient call of the wild sounds for him, he is bound to answer . . .

*

. . . the call still sounding in the depths of the forest . . . filled him with a great unrest and strange desires. It caused him to feel a vague, sweet gladness, and he was aware of wild yearnings and stirrings for he knew not what. Sometimes he pursued the call into the forest, looking for it as though it were a tangible thing, barking softly or defiantly, as the mood might dictate. He would thrust his nose into the cool wood moss, or into the black soil where long grasses grew, and snort with joy at the fat earth smells, or he would crouch for hours, as if in concealment, behind fungus-covered trunks of fallen trees, wide-eyed and wide-eared to all that moved and sounded about him. It might be, lying thus, that he hoped to surprise this call he could not understand. But he did not know why he did these various things. He was impelled to do them, and did not reason about them at all.

Irresistible impulses seized him. He would be lying in camp, dozing lazily in the heat of the day, when suddenly his head would lift and his ears cock up, intent and listening, and he would spring to his feet and dash away, and on and on, for hours, through the forest aisles and across the open spaces where the niggerheads bunched. He loved to run down dry watercourses, and to creep and spy upon the bird life in the woods. For a day at a time he would lie in the underbrush

31

where he could watch the partridges drumming and strutting up and down. But especially he loved to run in the dim twilight of the summer midnights, listening to the subdued and sleepy murmurs of the forest, reading signs and sounds as man may read a book, and seeking for the mysterious something that called – called, waking or sleeping, at all times, for him to come.

One night he sprang from sleep with a start, eager-eyed, nostrils quivering and scenting, his mane bristling in recurrent waves. From the forest came the call (or one note of it, for the call was many noted), distinct and definite as never before, – a long-drawn howl, like, yet unlike, any noise made by a husky dog. And he knew it, in the old familiar way, as a sound heard before. He sprang through the sleeping camp and in a swift silence dashed through the woods. As he drew closer to the cry he went more slowly, with caution in every movement, till he came to an open space among the trees, and looking out saw, erect on haunches, with nose pointed to the sky, a long, lean, timber wolf.

He had made no noise, yet it ceased from its howling and tried to sense his presence. Buck stalked into the open, half crouching, body gathered compactly together, tail straight and stiff, feet falling with unwonted care. Every movement advertised commingled threatening and overture of friendliness. It was the menacing truce that marks the meeting of wild beasts that prey. But the wolf fled at sight of him. He followed, with wild leapings, in a frenzy to overtake. He ran him into a blind channel, in the bed of the creek, where a timber jam barred the way. The wolf whirled about, pivoting on his hindlegs after the fashion of Joe and of all cornered husky dogs, snarling and bristling, clipping his teeth together in a continuous and rapid succession of snaps.

Buck did not attack, but circled him about and hedged him in with friendly advances. The wolf was suspicious and afraid; for Buck made three of him in weight, while his head barely reached Buck's shoulder. Watching his chance, he darted away, and the chase was resumed. Time and again he was cornered, and the thing repeated, though he was in poor condition, or Buck could not so easily have overtaken him. He would run until Buck's head was even with his flank, when he would whirl around at bay, only to dash away again at the first opportunity.

But in the end Buck's pertinacity was rewarded; for the wolf, finding that no harm was intended, finally sniffed noses with him. Then he became friendly, and played about in the nervous, half-coy way with which fierce beasts belie their fierceness. After some time of this the wolf started off at an easy lope in a manner that plainly showed he was going somewhere. He made it clear to Buck that he was to come, and they ran side by side through the sombre twilight, straight up the creek bed, into the gorge from which it issued, and across the bleak divide where it took its rise.

On the opposite slope of the watershed they came down into a level country where there were great stretches of forest and many streams, and through these great stretches they ran steadily, hour after hour, the sun rising higher and the day growing warmer. Buck was wildly glad. He knew he was at last answering the call, running by the side of his wood brother towards the place from where the call surely came. Old memories were coming upon him fast, and he was stirring to them as of old he stirred to the realities of which they were the shadows. He had done this thing before, somewhere in that other and dimly remembered world, and he was doing it again, now, running free in the open, the unpacked earth underfoot, the wide sky overhead.

They stopped by a running stream to drink, and, stopping, Buck remembered John Thornton. He sat down. The wolf started on towards the place from where the call surely came, then returned to him, sniffing noses and making actions as though to encourage him. But Buck turned about and started slowly on the back track. For the better part of an hour the wild brother ran by his side, whining softly. Then he sat down, pointed his nose upwards, and howled. It was a mournful howl, and as Buck held steadily on his way he heard it grow fainter and fainter until it was lost in the distance.

John Thornton was eating dinner when Buck dashed into camp and sprang upon him in a frenzy of affection, over-turning him, scrambling upon him, licking his face, biting

33

his hand – 'playing the general tom-fool', as John Thornton characterized it, the while he shook Buck back and forth and cursed him lovingly.

For two days and nights Buck never left camp, never let Thornton out of his sight. He followed him about at his work, watched him while he ate, saw him into his blankets at night and out of them in the morning. But after two days the call in the forest began to sound more imperiously than ever. Buck's restlessness came back on him, and he was haunted by recollections of the wild brother, and of the smiling land beyond the divide and the run side by side through the wide forest stretches. Once again he took to wandering in the woods, but the wild brother came no more; and though he listened through long vigils, the mournful howl was never raised.

He began to sleep out at night, staying away from camp for days at a time; and once he crossed the divide at the head of the creek and went down into the land of timber and streams. There he wandered for a week, seeking vainly for a fresh sign of the wild brother, killing his meat as he travelled and travelling with the long, easy lope that seems never to tire. He fished for salmon in a broad stream that emptied somewhere into the sea, and by this stream he killed a large black bear, blinded by the mosquitoes while likewise fishing, and raging through the forest helpless and terrible. Even so, it was a hard fight, and it aroused the last latent remnants of Buck's ferocity. And two days later, when he returned to his kill and found a dozen wolverines quarrelling over the spoil, he scattered them like chaff; and those that fled left two behind who would quarrel no more.

The blood-longing became stronger than ever before. He was a killer, a thing that preyed, living on the things that lived, unaided, alone, by virtue of his own strength and prowess, surviving triumphantly in a hostile environment where only the strong survived. Because of all this he became possessed of a great pride in himself, which communicated itself like a contagion to his physical being. It advertised itself in all his movements, was apparent in the play of every muscle, spoke plainly as speech in the way he carried himself, and made his glorious furry coat if anything more glorious. But for the stray brown on his muzzle and above his eyes, and for the splash of white hair that ran midmost down his chest, he might well have been mistaken for a gigantic wolf, larger than the largest of the breed. From his St Bernard father he had inherited size and weight, but it was his shepherd mother who had given shape to that size and weight. His muzzle was the long wolf muzzle, save that it was larger than the muzzle of any wolf; and his head, somewhat broader, was the wolf head on a massive scale.

His cunning was wolf cunning, and wild cunning; his intelligence, shepherd intelligence and St Bernard intelligence; and all this, plus an experience gained in the fiercest of schools, made him as formidable a creature as any that roamed the wild. A carnivorous animal, living on a straight meat diet, he was in full flower, at the high tide of his life, overspilling with vigour and virility. When Thornton passed a caressing hand along his back, a snapping and crackling followed the hand, each hair discharging its pent magnetism at the contact. Every part, brain and body, nerve tissue and fibre, was keyed to the most exquisite pitch; and between all the parts there was a perfect equilibrium or adjustment. To sights and sounds and events which required action, he responded with lightning-like rapidity. Quickly as a husky dog could leap to defend from attack or to attack, he could leap twice as quickly. He saw the movement, or heard sound, and responded in less time than another dog required to compass the mere seeing or hearing. He perceived and determined and responded in the same instant. In point of fact the three actions of perceiving, determining, and responding were sequential; but so infinitesimal were the intervals of time between them that they appeared simultaneous. His muscles were surcharged with vitality, and snapped into play sharply, like steel springs. Life streamed through him in splendid flood, glad and rampant, until it seemed that it would burst him asunder in sheer ecstasy and pour forth generously over the world.

'Never was there such a dog,' said John Thornton one day, as the partners watched Buck marching out of camp.

'When he was made, the mould was broke,' said Pete. 'Py jingo! I t'ink so mineself,' Hans affirmed.

They saw him marching out of camp, but they did not see the instant and terrible transformation which took place as soon as he was within the secrecy of the forest. He no longer marched. At once he became a thing of the wild, stealing along softly, cat-footed, a passing shadow that appeared and disappeared among the shadows. He knew how to take advantage of every cover, to crawl on his belly like a snake, and like a snake to leap and strike. He could take a ptarmigan from its nest, kill a rabbit as it slept, and snap in mid air the little chipmunks fleeing a second too late for the trees. Fish, in open pools, were not too quick for him; nor were beaver, mending their dams, too wary. He killed to eat, not from wantonness; but he preferred to eat what he killed himself. So a lurking humour ran through his deeds, and it was his delight to steal upon squirrels, and, when he all but had them, let them go, chattering in mortal fear to the tree-tops.

As the fall of the year came on, the moose appeared in greater abundance, moving slowly down to meet the winter in lower and less rigorous valleys. Buck had already dragged down a stray part-grown calf; but he wished strongly for larger and more formidable quarry, and he came upon it one day on the divide at the head of the creek. A band of twenty moose had crossed over from the land of streams and timber, and chief among them was a great bull. He was in a savage temper, and, standing over six feet from the ground, was as formidable an antagonist as even Buck could desire. Back and forth the bull tossed his great palmated antlers, branching to fourteen points and embracing seven feet within the tips. His small eyes burned with a vicious and bitter light, while he roared with fury at sight of Buck.

From the bull's side, just forward of the flank, protruded a feathered arrow-end, which accounted for his savageness. Guided by that instinct which came from the old hunting days of the primordial world, Buck proceeded to cut the bull out from the herd. It was no slight task. He would bark and dance about in front of the bull, just out of reach of the great antlers and of the terrible splay hooves which could have stamped

his life out with a single blow. Unable to turn his back on the fanged danger and go on, the bull would be driven into paroxysms of rage. At such moments he charged Buck, who retreated craftily, luring him on by a simulated inability to escape. But when he was thus separated from his fellows, two or three of the younger bulls would charge back upon Buck and enable the wounded bull to rejoin the herd.

There is a patience of the wild – dogged, tireless, persistent as life itself – that holds motionless for endless hours the spider in its web, the snake in its coils, the panther in its ambuscade; this patience belongs peculiarly to life when it hunts its living food; and it belonged to Buck as he clung to the flank of the herd, retarding its march, irritating the young bulls, worrying the cows with their half-grown calves, and driving the wounded bull mad with helpless rage. For half a day this continued. Buck multiplied himself, attacking from all sides, enveloping the herd in a whirlwind of menace, cutting out his victim as fast as it could rejoin its mates, wearing out the patience of creatures preyed upon, which is a lesser patience than that of creatures preying.

As the day wore along and the sun dropped to its bed in the northwest (darkness had come back and the fall nights were six hours long), the young bulls retraced their steps more and more reluctantly to the aid of their beset leader. The down-coming winter was harrying them on to the lower levels, and it seemed they could never shake off this tireless creature that held them back. Besides, it was not the life of the herd, or of the young bulls, that was threatened. The life of only one member was demanded, which was a remoter interest than their lives, and in the end they were content to pay the toll.

As twilight fell the old bull stood with lowered head, watching his mates – the cows he had known, the calves he had fathered, the bulls he had mastered – as they shambled on at a rapid pace through the fading light. He could not follow, for before his nose leaped the merciless fanged terror that would not let him go. Three hundredweight more than half a ton he weighed; he had lived a long, strong life, full of fight and struggle, and at the end he faced death at the teeth

38

of a creature whose head did not reach beyond his great knuckled knees.

From then on, night and day, Buck never left his prey, never gave it a moment's rest, never permitted it to browse the leaves of trees or the shoots of young birch and willow. Nor did he give the wounded bull opportunity to slake his burning thirst in the slender trickling streams they crossed. Often, in desperation, he burst into long stretches of flight. At such times Buck did not attempt to stay him, but loped easily at his heels, satisfied with the way the game was played, lying down when the moose stood still, attacking him fiercely when he strove to eat or drink.

The great head drooped more and more under its tree of horns, and the shambling trot grew weaker and weaker. He took to standing for long periods, with nose to the ground and dejected ears dropped limply; and Buck found more time in which to get water for himself and in which to rest. At such moments, panting with red lolling tongue and with eyes fixed upon the big bull, it appeared to Buck that a change was coming over the face of things. He could feel a new stir in the land. As the moose were coming into the land, other kinds of life were coming in. Forest and stream and air seemed palpitant with their presence. The news of it was borne in upon him, not by sight, sound or smell, but by some other subtler sense. He heard nothing, saw nothing, yet knew that the land was somehow different; that through it strange things were afoot and ranging; and he resolved to investigate after he had finished the business in hand.

At last, at the end of the fourth day, he pulled the great moose down. For a day and a night he remained by the kill, eating and sleeping, turn and turn about. Then, rested, refreshed and strong, he turned his face toward camp and John Thornton. He broke into a long easy lope, and went on, hour after hour, never at loss for the tangled way, heading straight home through strange country with a certitude of direction that put man and his magnetic needle to shame.

As he held on he became more and more conscious of the new stir in the land. There was life abroad in it different from the life which had been there throughout the summer. No longer was this fact borne in upon him in some subtle, mysterious way. The birds talked of it, the squirrels chattered about it, the very breeze whispered of it. Several times he stopped and drew in the fresh morning air in great sniffs, reading a message which made him leap on with greater speed. He was oppressed with a sense of calamity happening, if it were not calamity already happened; and as he crossed the last watershed and dropped down into the valley towards camp, he proceeded with greater caution.

Three miles away he came upon a fresh trail that sent his neck hair rippling and bristling. It led straight towards camp and John Thornton. Buck hurried on, swiftly and stealthily, every nerve straining and tense, alert to the multitudinous details which told a story – all but the end. His nose gave him a varying description of the passage of the life on the heels of which he was travelling. He remarked the pregnant silence of the forest. The bird life had flitted. The squirrels were hiding. One only he saw, a sleek grey fellow, flattened against a grey dead limb so that he seemed part of it, a woody excrescence upon the wood itself.

As Buck slid along with the obscureness of a gliding shadow, his nose was jerked suddenly to the side as though a positive force had gripped and pulled it. He followed the new scent into a thicket and found Nig. He was lying on his side, dead where he had dragged himself, an arrow protruding, head and feathers, from either side of his body.

A hundred yards farther on, Buck came upon one of the sled-dogs Thornton had bought in Dawson. This dog was thrashing about in a death-struggle, directly on the trail, and Buck passed around him without stopping. From the camp came the faint sound of many voices, rising and falling in a sing-song chant. Bellying forward to the edge of the clearing, he found Hans, lying on his face, feathered with arrows like a porcupine. At the same instant Buck peered out where the spruce-bough lodge had been and saw what made his hair leap straight up on his neck and shoulders. A gust of overpowering rage swept over him. He did not know that he growled, but he growled aloud with a terrible ferocity. For the last time in his life he allowed passion to usurp cunning

40

and reason, and it was because of his great love for John Thornton that he lost his head.

The Yeehats were dancing about the wreckage of the spruce-bough lodge when they heard a fearful roaring and saw rushing upon them an animal the like of which they had never seen before. It was Buck, a live hurricane of fury, hurling himself upon them in a frenzy to destroy. He sprang at the foremost man (it was the chief of the Yeehats), ripping the throat wide open till the rent jugular spouted a fountain of blood. He did not pause to worry the victim, but ripped in passing, with the next bound tearing wide the throat of a second man. There was no withstanding him. He plunged about in their very midst, tearing, rending, destroying, in constant and terrific motion which defied the arrows they discharged at him. In fact, so inconceivably rapid were his movements, and so closely were the Indians tangled together, that they shot one another with the arrows; and one young hunter, hurling a spear at Buck in mid-air, drove it through the chest of another hunter, with such force that the point broke through the skin of the back and stood out beyond. Then a panic seized the Yeehats, and they fled in terror to the woods, proclaiming as they fled the advent of the Evil Spirit.

And truly Buck was the Fiend incarnate, raging at their heels and dragging them down like deer as they raced through the trees. It was a fateful day for the Yeehats. They scattered far and wide over the country, and it was not till a week later that the last of the survivors gathered together in a lower valley and counted their losses. As for Buck, wearying of the pursuit, he returned to the desolated camp. He found Peter where he had been killed in his blankets in the first moment of surprise. Thornton's desperate struggle was fresh-written on the earth, and Buck scented every detail of it down to the edge of a deep pool. By the end, head and fore-feet in the water, lay Skeet, faithful to the last. The pool itself, muddy and discoloured from the sluice boxes, effectually hid what it contained, and it contained John Thornton; for Buck followed his trace into the water, from which no trace led away.

All day Buck brooded by the pool or roamed restlessly about the camp. Death, as a cessation of movement, as a passing out and away from the lives of the living, he knew, and he knew John Thornton was dead. It left a great void in him, somewhat akin to hunger, but a void which ached and ached, and which food could not fill. At times when he paused to contemplate the carcasses of the Yeehats, he forgot the pain of it; and at such times he was aware of a great pride in himself – a pride greater than any he had yet experienced. He had killed man, the noblest game of all, and he had killed in the face of the law of club and fang. He sniffed the bodies curiously. They had died so easily. It was harder to kill a husky dog than them. They were no match at all, were it not for their arrows and spears and clubs. Thenceforward he would be unafraid of them except when they bore in their hands their arrows, spears and clubs.

Night came on, and a full moon rose high over the trees into the sky, lighting the land till it lay bathed in ghostly day. And with the coming of the night, brooding and mourning by the pool, Buck became alive to a stirring of the new life in the forest other than that which the Yeehats had made. He stood up, listening and scenting. From far away drifted a faint, sharp yelp, followed by a chorus of similar sharp yelps. As the moments passed the yelps grew closer and louder. Again Buck knew them as things heard in that other world which persisted in his memory. He walked to the centre of the open space and listened. It was the call, the many-noted call, sounding more luringly and compellingly than ever before. And as never before, he was ready to obey. John Thornton was dead. The last tie was broken. Man and the claims of man no longer bound him.

Hunting their living meat, as the Yeehats were hunting it, on the flanks of the migrating moose, the wolf-pack had at last crossed over from the land of streams and timber and invaded Buck's valley. Into the clearing where the moonlight streamed, they poured in a silvery flood; and in the centre of the clearing stood Buck, motionless as a statue, waiting their coming. They were awed, so still and large he stood, and a moment's pause fell, till the boldest one leaped straight for him. Like a flash Buck struck, breaking the neck. Then he stood, without movement, as before, the stricken wolf rolling in agony behind him. Three others tried it in sharp succession; and one after the other they drew back, streaming blood from slashed throats or shoulders.

This was sufficient to fling the whole pack forward, pell-mell, crowded together, blocked and confused by its eagerness to pull down the prey. Buck's marvellous quickness and agility stood him in good stead. Pivoting on his hindlegs, and snapping and gashing, he was everywhere at once, presenting a front which was apparently unbroken so swiftly did he whirl and guard from side to side. But to prevent them from getting behind him, he was forced to back, down past the pool and into the creek bed, till he brought up against a high gravel bank. He worked along to a right angle in the bank which the men had made in the course of mining, and in this angle he came to bay, protected on three sides and with nothing to do but face the front.

And so well did he face it, that at the end of half an hour the wolves drew back discomfited. The tongues of all were out and lolling, the white fangs showing cruelly white in the moonlight. Some were lying down with heads raised and ears pricked forward; others stood on their feet, watching him; and still others were lapping water from the pool. One wolf, long and lean and grey, advanced cautiously, in a friendly manner, and Buck recognized the wild brother with whom he had run for a night and a day. He was whining softly, and, as Buck whined, they touched noses.

Then an old wolf, gaunt and battle-scarred, came forward. Buck writhed his lips into the preliminary of a snarl, but sniffed noses with him. Whereupon the old wolf sat down, pointed nose at the moon, and broke out the long wolf howl. The others sat down and howled. And now the call came to Buck in unmistakable accents. He, too, sat down and howled. This over, he came out of his angle and the pack crowded around him, sniffing in half-friendly, half-savage manner. The leaders lifted the yelp of the pack and sprang away into the woods. The wolves swung in behind, yelping in chorus. And Buck ran with them, side by side with the wild brother, yelping as he ran.

(from *The Call of the Wild,* 1903)

Captives

Auguries of Innocence

A robin redbreast in a cage
Puts all heaven in a rage...
The wild deer wand'ring here and there
Keeps the human soul from care.

WILLIAM BLAKE

Song

I had a dove and the sweet dove died;
  And I have thought it died of grieving:
O, what could it grieve for? Its feet were tied
  With a silken thread of my own hand's weaving;
Sweet little red feet! Why did you die –
Why should you leave me, sweet bird! Why?
You lived alone in the forest tree,
Why, pretty thing! would you not live with me?
I kissed you oft and gave you white peas:
Why not live sweetly, as in the green trees?

JOHN KEATS

The Hawk

'Call down the hawk from the air:
Let him be hooded or caged
Till the yellow eye has grown mild;
For larder and spit are bare,
The old cook enraged,
The scullion gone wild.'

'I will not be clapped in a hood,
Nor a cage, nor alight upon wrist,
Now I have learnt to be proud
Hovering over the wood
In the broken mist
Or tumbling cloud...'

W. B. YEATS

Hawk Roosting

I sit in the top of the wood, my eyes closed.
Inaction, no falsifying dream
Between my hooked head and hooked feet:
Or in sleep rehearse perfect kills and eat.

The convenience of the high trees!
The air's buoyancy and the sun's ray
Are of advantage to me;
And the earth's face upward for my inspection.

My feet are locked upon the rough bark.
It took the whole of Creation
To produce my foot, my each feather:
Now I hold Creation in my foot

Or fly up, and revolve it all slowly –
I kill where I please because it is all mine.
There is no sophistry in my body:
My manners are tearing off heads –

The allotment of death.
For the one path of my flight is direct
Through the bones of the living.
No arguments assert my right:

The sun is behind me.
Nothing has changed since I began.
My eye has permitted no change.
I am going to keep things like this.

TED HUGHES

Trees in the Moonlight

Trees in the moonlight stand
  Still as a steeple,
And so quiet they seem like ghosts
  Of country people.

Dead farmers and their wives
  Of long, long ago,
Haunting the countryside
  They used to know;

Old gossips and talkers
  With tongues gone still;
Ploughmen rooted in the land
  They used to till;

Old carters and harvesters,
  Their wheels long rotten;
Old maids whose very names
  Time has forgotten.

Ghosts are they hereabouts;
  Them the moon sees,
Dark and still in the fields
  Like sleeping trees.

Long nights in autumn
  Hear them strain and cry,
Torn with a wordless sorrow
  As the gale sweeps by.

Spring makes fresh buds appear
  On the old boughs,
As if it could to their old wishes
  These ghosts arouse.

Trees in the summer night
  By moonlight linger on
So quiet they seem like ghosts
  Of people gone,

And it would be small wonder
　　If at break of day
They heard the far-off cock-crow
　　And fled away.

JAMES REEVES

The Noble Nature

It is not growing like a tree
In bulk, doth make Man better be;
Or standing long an oak, three hundred year,
To fall a log at last, dry, bald, and sere:
　　A lily of a day
　　Is fairer far in May,
Although it fall and die that night;
It was the plant and flower of Light.
In small proportions we just beauties see;
And in short measures life may perfect be.

BEN JONSON

47

The Natural History of Selborne

GILBERT WHITE

Gilbert White, who wrote what was first called The Natural History and Antiquities of Selborne in the County of South- ampton, *was born in the house of his grandfather, the vicar of Selborne, in 1720. This place remained to him the dearest on earth. He became a parson himself, but by peculiarities of church administration could never be vicar of Selborne, since the living was in the gift of Magdalen College, Oxford, while Gilbert White was a fellow of Oriel College. However, he was able to accept the curacy of Selborne, and later to live there until his death, administering the parish in the permanent absence of the appointed incumbent.*

Gilbert White died in 1793, at the age of 73, having seen his Natural History of Selborne *published five years earlier. Few men have written with such gentle authority; his love of the smallest aspect of wildlife, his unflagging curiosity and trium- phant conclusions give him a permanent place among English nature writers.*

*

The Royal Forest of Wolmer is a tract of land of about seven miles in length, by two and a half in breadth, running nearly from north to south, and is abutted on, to begin to the south and so proceed eastward, by the parishes of Greatham, Lysse, Rogate and Trotton, in the county of Sussex; by Bramshot, Hedleigh and Kingsly. This royalty consists en- tirely of sand covered with heath and fern; but is somewhat diversified with hills and dales, without having one standing tree in the whole extent. In the bottoms, where the waters stagnate, are many bogs which formerly abounded with sub- terraneous trees ... I myself have seen cottages on the verge of this wild district, whose timbers consisted of a black hard wood, looking like oak, which the owners assured me they procured from the bogs by probing the soil with spits, or some such instruments: but the peat is so much cut out, and the moors have been so well examined that none has been found of late. Besides the oak, I have also been shown pieces of fossil-wood of a paler colour, and softer nature, which the inhabitants call fir: but, upon a nice examination, and trial by fire, I could discover nothing resinous in them; and therefore rather suppose that they were parts of a willow or alder, or some such aquatic tree.

This lonely domain is a very agreeable haunt for many sorts of wild fowls, which not only frequent it in the winter, but breed there in the summer; such as lapwings, snipes, wild-ducks, and, as I have discovered within these few years, teals. Partridges in vast plenty are bred in good seasons on the verge of this forest, into which they love to make excursions: and in particular in the dry summer of 1740 and 1741, and some years after, they swarmed to such a degree, that parties of unreasonable sportsmen killed twenty and sometimes thirty brace in a day.

But there was a nobler species of game in this forest, now extinct, which I have heard old people say abounded much before shooting flying became so common, and that was the heath-cock, black game, or grouse. When I was a little boy I recollect one coming now and then to my father's table.

The last pack remembered was killed about thirty-five years ago; and within these ten years one solitary greyhen was sprung by some beagles in beating for a hare . . .

Nor does the loss of our black game prove the only gap in the *Fauna Selborniensis*; for another beautiful link in the chain of beings is wanting, I mean the red deer which toward the beginning of this century amounted to about five hundred head, and made a stately appearance. There is an old keeper, now alive, named Adams, whose great-grandfather (mentioned in a perambulation taken in 1635), grandfather, father and self, enjoyed the head keepership of Wolmer-forest in succession for more than a hundred years. This person assures me, that his father has often told him, that Queen Anne, as she was journeying on the Portsmouth road, did not think the forest of Wolmer beneath her royal regard. For she came out of the great road at Lippock, which is just by, and reposing herself on a bank smoothed for that purpose, lying about half a mile to the east of Wolmer-pond, and still called Queen's-bank, saw with great complacency and satisfaction the whole herd of red deer brought by the keepers along the vale before her, consisting then of about five hundred head. A sight, this, worthy the attention of the greatest sovereign! But he further adds that, by means of the Waltham blacks [*a gang of thieves and poachers of the day, often with blacked faces, against whom stern legal action was eventually taken*], or to use his own expression, as soon as they began *blacking*, they were reduced to about fifty head, and so continued decreasing until the time of the late Duke of Cumberland. It is now more than thirty years ago that his highness sent down an huntsman, and six yeoman-prickers, in scarlet jackets laced with gold, attended by the stag-hounds; ordering them to take every deer in this forest alive, and convey them in carts to Windsor. In the course of the summer they caught every stag, some of which showed extraordinary diversion; but, in the following winter, when the hinds were also carried off, such fine chases were exhibited as served the country people for matter of talk and wonder for years afterwards. I saw myself one of the yeomen-prickers single out a stag from the herd, and must confess it was the most curious feat of activity I ever beheld, superior to anything in Mr Astley's riding-school. The exertions made by the horse and deer much exceeded all my expectations; though the former greatly excelled the latter in speed. When the devoted deer was separated from his companions, they gave him, by their watches, law, as they called it, for twenty minutes; when, sounding their horns, the stop-dogs were permitted to pursue, and a most gallant scene ensued . . .

Our old race of deer-stealers are hardly extinct yet; it was but a little while ago that, over their ale, they used to recount the exploits of their youth; such as watching the pregnant hind to her lair and, when the calf was dropped, paring its feet with a penknife to the quick to prevent its escape, till it was large and fat enough to be killed; the shooting at one of their neighbours in a turnip-field by moonshine, mistaking him for a deer; and losing a dog in the following extra-ordinary manner: Some fellows, suspecting that a calf new-fallen was deposited in a certain spot of thick fern, went, with a lurcher, to surprise it; when the parent hind rushed out of the brake, and, taking a vast spring with all her feet close together, pitched upon the neck of the dog, and broke it short in two.

Another temptation to idleness and sporting was a number of rabbits, which possessed all the hillocks and dry places; but these being inconvenient to the huntsmen, on account of their burrows, when they came to take away the deer, they permitted the country people to destroy them all.

Such forests and wastes, when their allurements to irregularities are removed, are of considerable service to neighbourhoods that verge upon them, by furnishing them with peat and turf for their firing; with fuel for the burning their lime; and with ashes for their grasses; and by main-taining their geese and their stock of young cattle at little or no expense . . .

Though (by statutes 4 and 5 W. and M. c.23) 'to burn on any waste, between Candlemas and Midsummer, any grig, ling, heath and furze, goss or fern, is punishable with whip-ping and confinement to the house of correction', yet, in this forest, about March or April, according to the dryness of the season, such vast heath-fires are lighted up, that they often get to a masterless head, and, catching the hedges, have sometimes been communicated to the underwoods, woods and coppices, where great damage has ensued. The plea for these burnings is, that, when the old coat of heath, etc., is consumed, young will sprout up, and afford much tender browse for cattle; but, where there is large old furze, the fire, following the roots, consumes the very ground; so that for hundreds of acres nothing is to be seen but smother and desolation; the whole circuit round seen like the cinders of a volcano; and the soil being quite exhausted, no traces of vegetation are to be found for years . . .

*

O Sweet Woods the Delight of Solitariness!

O sweet woods the delight of solitariness!
O how much do I like your solitariness!
Here nor treason is hid, vailed in innocence,
Nor envies snaky eye finds any harbour here,
Nor flatterers venomous insinuations,
Nor coming humorists puddled opinions,
Nor courteous ruin of proffered usury,
Nor time prattled away, cradle of ignorance,
Nor causeless duty, nor cumber of arrogance,
Nor trifling title of vanity dazzleth us,
Nor golden manacles stand for a paradise.
Here wrong's name is unheard; slander a monster is;
Keep thy spirit from abuse, here no abuse doth haunt,
What man grafts in a tree dissimulation?

SIR PHILIP SIDNEY

Under the Greenwood Tree

Under the greenwood tree
Who loves to lie with me,
And turn his merry note
Unto the sweet bird's throat,
Come hither, come hither, come hither:
Here shall he see
No enemy
But winter and rough weather.

Who doth ambition shun,
And loves to live i' the sun,
Seeking the food he eats,
And pleased with what he gets,
Come hither, come hither, come hither:
Here shall he see
No enemy
But winter and rough weather.

(from *As You Like It*)   WILLIAM SHAKESPEARE

The Red Scourge of the Forest

CHARLES G. D. ROBERTS

Charles G. D. Roberts was born in Canada in 1860, and died after a long and varied life in 1943. He was a teacher, a poet, a journalist among other things – but his fame rests on his books about animals and birds. He writes in a slightly old-fashioned but vivid style. His love of his subject may be summed up in the phrase he uses so often – he calls animals and birds the wild kindred, *which is as nice a description of the relationship as any I have heard.*

*

[Red Fox, with his mate and his cubs, faces a terror he has never known before . . .]

When the drought had grown almost unbearable, and man and beast, herb and tree, all seemed to hold up hands of appeal together to the brazen sky, crying out, 'How long? How long?' there came at last a faint, acrid pungency on the air which made the dry woods shudder with fear. Close on the heels of this fierce, menacing smell came a veil of thinnest vapour, lilac-toned, delicate, magical, and indescribably sinister. Sky and trees, hills and fields, they took on a new beauty under this light, transfiguring touch. But the touch was one that made all the forest folk, and the settlement folk as well, scan the horizon anxiously and calculate the direction of the wind.

Miles away, far down the wooded ridges and beyond the farthest of the little lakes to southward, some irresponsible and misbegotten idiot had gone away and left his camp-fire burning. Eating its way furtively through the punk-dry turf, and moss, and dead-leaf debris, the fire had spread undiscovered over an area of considerable width, and had at last begun to lay hold upon the trees. On an almost imperceptible wind, one morning the threatening pungency stole up over the settlement and the ridge. Later in the day the thinnest of the smoke-veil arrived. And that night, had anyone been on watch on the top of the ridge, where Red Fox had had his lookout two months earlier, he might have discerned a thread of red light, cut here and there with slender, sharp tongues of flame, along a section of the southward sky. Only the eagles, however, saw this beautiful, ominous sight. In the last of the twilight they rose and led off their two nestlings – now clothed with loose black feathers, and looking nearly as large as their parents – to the top of a naked cliff far up on the flank of old Ringwaak. Here they all four huddled together on a safe ledge, and watched the disastrous red light with fascinated eyes.

Red Fox, meanwhile, was in his lair, too troubled and apprehensive to go hunting. He had had no experience of that scourge of the drought-stricken woods, the forest fire. His instinct gave him sufficient information on the subject,

at least at this early stage of the emergency. And for once his keen sagacity found itself at fault. He could do nothing but wait.

As the night deepened a wind arose and the red line across the southern horizon became a fierce glow that mounted into the sky, with leaping spires of flame along its lower edge. The wind quickly grew into a gale, driving the smoke and flame before it. Soon a doe and two fawns, their eyes wide with terror, went bounding past Red Fox. Still he made no stir, for he wanted to know more about the peril that threatened him before he decided which way to flee to escape it. As he pondered – no longer resting under his bush, but standing erect behind his den mouth, his mate and the youngsters crouching near and trembling – a clumsy porcupine rattled past, at a pace of which Red Fox would never have believed a porcupine capable. Then a weasel, – and four or five rabbits immediately at its heels, all unmindful of its insatiable ferocity. By this time the roar and savage crackle of the flames came clearly down the wind, with puffs of choking smoke. It was plainly time to do something. Red Fox decided that it was hopeless to flee straight ahead of the flames, which would be sure to outrace and outwind his family in a short time. He thought it best to run at a slant across the conflagration, and so, if possible, get beyond the skirts of it. He thought of the open fields adjoining the settlement, and made up his mind that there lay the best chance of safety. With a sharp signal to his mate, he started on a long diagonal across the meadow, over the brook, and down the hill, the whole family keeping close behind him. No sooner had they crossed it than the meadow was suddenly alive with fleeing shapes, – deer, and a bear, woodchucks, squirrels, and rabbits, two wildcats, and mice, weasels and porcupines. There were no muskrats or mink because these latter were keeping close to the watercourses, however shrunken, and putting their trust in these for final escape.

As Red Fox ran on his cunning cross line, he suddenly saw the red tongues licking through the trees ahead of him, while blazing brands and huge sparks began to drop about him. The air was full of appalling sights and sounds. Seeing that the fire had cut him off, he turned and ran on another diagonal, hoping to escape over the ridge. For a little while he sped thus, cutting across the stream of wild-eyed fugitives, but presently found that in this direction also the flames had headed him. Checked straight behind his den by a long stretch of hardwood growth, the flames had gone far ahead on either flank, tearing through the dry balsamy fir and spruce groves. Not understanding the properties of that appalling element, fire, nor guessing that it preferred some kinds of woods to others, Red Fox had been misled in his calculations. There was nothing now for him to do but join the ordinary, panic-stricken throng of fugitives, and flee straight ahead.

In this frightful and uncomprehended situation, however, Red Fox kept his wits about him. He remembered that about a mile ahead, a little lower down, there was a swamp on a kind of hillside plateau, and a fair-sized beaver pond at the farther end of it. Swerving somewhat to the left, he led the way towards this possible refuge, at the utmost speed of which his family were capable. This speed, of course, was regulated by the pace of the weakest members; and for the big, headstrong whelp, whom his father had had to save from the old raccoon and from the mad muskrat, it was by no means fast enough. Terrified, but at the same time independent and self-confident, he darted ahead, neck and neck with a bunch of rabbits and a weasel, none of whom appeared to have the slightest objection to his company. To his mother's urgent calls he paid no heed whatever, and in a moment he had vanished. Whether his strength and blind luck pulled him through, or whether he perished miserably, overtaken by the flames, Red Fox never knew.

Keeping very close together, the diminished family sped on, bellies to earth, through the strange, hushed rustle of the silently fleeing wild creatures. Behind them the crackling roar of the fire deepened rapidly, while the dreadful glow of the sky seemed to lean forward as if to topple upon them. From time to time the smoke volleyed thicker about them, as if to strangle and engulf them. Over their heads flew hundreds of panic-blinded birds – grouse, and woodpeckers, and the smaller sparrow and warbler tribes. But the wiser crows, with the hawks and owls, knew enough to fly high into the air beyond the clutch of the flames.

Comparing the speed of his own flight with that of the flames behind him, Red Fox felt that he would make the beaver pond in time, though with nothing to spare. His compact little party was now joined by two raccoons, whose pace seemed to just equal that of the young foxes. For some reason they seemed to recognize a confident leadership in Red Fox, and felt safer in following him than in trusting to their own resources. Yet, unlike most of the fugitives, they appeared to be in no sense panic-stricken. Their big, keen, restless eyes took note of everything and wore a look of brave self-possession. They were not going to lose in this race of life and death through any failure of theirs to grasp opportunity. Had Red Fox lost his head and done anything to discredit his leadership, they would have promptly parted company with him.

The swift procession of fear surrounding Red Fox and his family was continually changing, though always the same in its headlong, bewildering confusion. Some of the creatures, such as the deer and the rabbits, were swifter than the fox family, and soon left them behind. Once, indeed, a wildly bounding doe, belated somehow, going through the thickets with great leaps of thirty feet from hoof-mark to hoof-mark, brought her sharp hooves down within a hair's breadth of Red Fox's nose, so that he felt himself lucky to have escaped with a whole hide. Others of the animals, on the other hand, were slower than the fox family, and were soon outstripped, to fall back into the galloping vortex whose heat was already searching hungrily under the thickets far ahead. The porcupines, for instance, and the woodchucks, and the skunks – hopeless but self-possessed in the face of fate, – could not keep up the terrible pace, and soon went under. All this tragedy, however, was no concern of Red Fox, who troubled himself not a jot about anyone's business but that of his own family, where his interest, in a moment such as this, began and ended.

Suddenly, to his intense astonishment, he ran plump into a big black bear, who stood motionless in a hollow under a thick-leaved beech-tree. Red Fox could not understand why she was not fleeing like the rest of the world. But as he swerved aside, he saw behind her, stretched out in utter exhaustion, her two cubs. Then he understood. She had evidently brought her cubs a long way, the little animals running till they could not stumble one step more: and now, having exhausted every effort to arouse them and urge them farther, she was awaiting her doom quietly, holding her great black body to shield them as long as possible from the onrush of the flame. The fugitives streamed past her on either side, but she saw none of them, as her eyes, strained with despair, wandered back and forth between the roaring blaze and the prostrate bodies of her cubs.

Red Fox noted with anxiety his own youngsters were beginning to slacken speed and stumble as they ran, requiring all their mother's watchful efforts to keep them spurred on. But a moment later he caught a red gleam reflected from the water just ahead. He smelled the water, too; and the wearying puppies, as they smelled it, were encouraged to a fresh burst of speed. A few seconds more and they were up to their necks in the saving coolness, and the two raccoons close beside them, and every kind of forest dweller panting and splashing around them.

Much as they hated the water, the fox family could swim in such an emergency as this; and Red Fox led the way out to the biggest beaver-house, which stood, a ragged dome of sticks and mud, near the centre of the pond. There was trampling and splashing and swimming everywhere, most of the larger animals, the bears and deer, gathering at the farther side of the pond. On several overhanging limbs crouched wildcats and a couple of lynxes, afraid to take to the water, which they abhorred. Amid all the confusion and terrifying sounds, the beavers, usually the shyest of wild creatures, were working imperturbably, paying no heed whatever to the motley throngs scurrying around them. They knew that the long drought had baked the roofs of their houses to tinder, and now, in a desperate but well-ordered haste, they were covering them in wet mud from the bottom of the pond. They, at least, were going to be safe.

By this time the heat was extreme, and the crackling roar

of the flames was almost upon them. Red Fox led his family to the farthest side of the big beaver-house, but himself kept watch where he could see everything. The smoke was now volleying down upon the surface of the pond in great bursts, the water was smitten here and there with red brands that hissed as they fell, and the tongues of flame that ran up the tall trunks of pine and fir seemed to leap bodily into the air in order to set fire to the trees ahead of them. The whole southeastern sky was now like a wall of molten and blazing copper, stretching to the zenith and about to topple down the world. Against it, a last despairing barrier already beginning to crumble, stood black and defiant the water-side fringe of trees.

At last the too frail barrier went down, and the roaring storm of fire broke full upon the pond. In their pain and panic, many of the creatures trampled one another under water. Others, afraid of drowning, were slain by the implacable heat. The fox family, however, well away from the densest and the maddest of the crowd, sank their bodies quite under water, just lifting their noses every other second to breathe. Red Fox himself, resolutely curious no matter what the emergency, kept his head above water as long as possible and dipped it under as briefly as possible, enduring the heat till his eyes felt scorched and his nostrils almost blistered, in order that he might be aware of all that happened. He saw one great lynx, his fur so singed that he looked hardly half his usual size, spring far out into the water with a screech, and never rise again. He saw the other great cats swimming frantically, and clambering out of the unaccustomed element upon the backs of bears and deer, who paid no attention to their strangely unhostile burdens. One huge wildcat, badly scorched, succeeded in reaching the top of the beaver-house, where he crouched snarling and spitting at the flames, while squirrels and chipmunks crowded about him unheeded. Drenched from his plunge, his thick wet fur seemed to withstand the heat for a time. Then his wits came to his help and he slunk down into the water again, his eyes staring wide with the very madness of terror.

In a minute or two the flames had raced round both sides

of the pond and met again, enclosing the pond with a spouting and roaring wall of fire. The rabble of beasts gathered at the farther side now surged frantically back towards the centre of the pond; and Red Fox anxiously made ready to lead his family away from the path of the bedlam mob. But the unhappy creatures, too crushed together to swim, merely trod one another down, and most of them were drowned long before they reached the centre. The bigger and stronger ones of course survived the struggle, but of these many presently went down, burned inwardly by the flames they had inhaled; and the assault which Red Fox had dreaded was utterly broken. Only a few stragglers reached the beaver-houses in the centre, where the wet mud was sending up clouds of steam.

The pond was no longer crowded, but looked almost deserted in the furious crimson glow, for all the survivors were either swimming about the centre, diving every other moment to keep their heads from scorching, or else crouched like Red Fox beneath the sheltering element. Only the wise beavers were perfectly content within their water-houses, and the muskrats in their deep holes, and the mink lurking under the swampy overhanging banks.

In a few minutes more the heat palpably diminished, as the underbrush, branches and smaller trees along the windward shore of the pond burned themselves out in the fierce wind, leaving only the taller trunks to flare and flicker like half-spent torches. The heat from the roaring underbrush of the leeward side, of course, was partly carried away by the wind. Little by little the centre of the conflagration shifted ahead, and the leaping spires of flame moved forward, leaving behind them thick smoke, and red glowing spikes and pillars of hot coal to illuminate the dark. The remnants of the bushes along the shore still snapped with vivid and spiteful sparks, and the thick moss and leaf-mould that matted the forest floor smouldered like glowing peat. As the heat further moderated, many of the animals still left alive tried to go ashore, but only succeeded in burning their feet. Red Fox, too sagacious for such a vain attempt, led his family out upon the top of the beaver-house and waited philosophically for the awful night to wear away. At last, after hours that seemed like months, the savage glow in the northeastern sky began to pale in the approach of dawn, and pure streamers of saffron and tender pink stole out across the dreadful desolation. By noon, though the fire still ate its way in the moss, and the smarting smoke still rose thickly on every side, and here and there the blackened rampikes still flickered fitfully, the ruined woods were cool enough for Red Fox to lead his family through them by picking his way very carefully. Working over towards his right, he came at last, footsore and singed and choked with thirst, to the first of the lower pastures, which had proved too wide for the flames to cross. On the other side of the pasture were woods, still green, shadowy, unscarred. In a sort of ecstasy the foxes sped across the hillocky pasture and plunged into the blessed cool.

(from *Red Fox*, 1905)

The Vixen

Among the taller woods with ivy hung,
The old fox plays and dances round her young.
She snuffs and barks if any passes by
And swings her tail and turns prepared to fly.
The horseman hurries by, she bolts to see,
And turns agen, from danger never free.
If any stands she runs among the poles
And barks and snaps and drives them in the holes.
The shepherd sees them and the boy goes by
And gets a stick and progs the hole to try.
They get all still and lie in safety sure,
And out again when everything's secure,
And start and snap at blackbirds bouncing by
To fight and catch the great white butterfly.

JOHN CLARE

The Hollow Wood

Out in the sun the goldfinch flits
Along the thistle-tops, flits and twits
Above the hollow wood
Where birds swim like fish –
Fish that laugh and shriek –
To and fro, far below
In the pale hollow wood.

Lichen, ivy, and moss
Keep evergreen the trees
That stand half-flayed and dying,
And the dead trees on their knees
In dog's-mercury and moss:
And the bright twit of the goldfinch drops
Down there as he flits on thistle-tops.

EDWARD THOMAS

Rural Rides

WILLIAM COBBETT

What, in point of beauty, is a country without woods and lofty trees?

*

Bollitree Castle, Herefordshire
Wednesday, 14 November 1821

Rode to the Forest of Dean, up a very steep hill. The lanes here are between high banks, and, on the sides of the hills, the road is a rock, the water having, long ago, washed all the earth away. Pretty works are, I find, carried on here, as is the case in all the other *public forests*! Are these things *always* to be carried on in this way? Here is a domain of thirty thousand acres of the finest timber-land in the world, and with coal-mines endless! Is this *worth nothing*? Cannot each acre yield ten trees a year? Are not these trees worth a pound apiece? Is not the estate worth three or four hundred thousand pounds a year? And does it yield *anything to the public*, to whom it belongs? But it is useless to waste one's breath in this way. We must have a *reform of the Parliament*: without it the whole thing will fall to pieces. The only good purpose that these forests offer is that of furnishing a place of being to labourers' families on their skirts; and here their cottages are very neat, and the people look hearty and well, just as they do round the forests in Hampshire. Every cottage has a pig, or two. These graze in the forest, and, in the fall, eat acorns and beech-nuts and the seed of the ash; for, these last, as well as the others, are very full of oil, and a pig that is put to his shifts will pick the seed very nicely out from the husks. Some of these foresters keep cows, and all of them have bits of ground, cribbed, of course, at different times, from the forest: and to what better use can the ground be put? I saw

64

several wheat stubbles from 40 rods to 10 rods. I asked one man how much wheat he had from about 10 rods. He said more than two bushels. Here is bread for three weeks, or more, perhaps; and a winter's straw for the pigs besides. Are these things nothing? . . .

Kensington
Friday, 4 January 1822

. . . I cannot quit Battle without observing that the country is very pretty all about it. All hill or valley. A great deal of woodland, in which the underwood is generally very fine, though the oaks are not very fine, and a good deal covered with *moss* . . . Woodland countries are interesting on many accounts. Not so much on account of their masses of green leaves, as on account of the variety of sights and sounds and incidents that they afford. Even in winter the coppices are beautiful to the eye, while they comfort the mind with the idea of shelter and warmth. In spring they change their hue from day to day during two whole months, which is about the

time from the first appearance of the delicate leaves of the birch to the full expansion of those of the ash; and even before the leaves come at all to intercept the view, what in the vegetable creation is so delightful to behold as the bed of a coppice bespangled with primroses and bluebells? The opening of the birch leaves is the signal for the pheasant to begin to crow, for the blackbird to whistle, and the thrush to sing; and just when the oak-buds begin to look reddish, and not a day before, the whole tribe of finches burst forth in songs from every bough, while the lark, imitating them all, carries the joyous sounds to the sky . . .

The Insect World

The insect world amid the suns and dew
Awake and hum their tiny songs anew,
And climb the totter-grass and blossom's stem
As huge in size as mighty oaks to them;
And rushy burnets on the pasture rise
As tall as castles to their little eyes;
Each leaf's a town and the smooth meadow grass
A mighty world whose bounds they never pass;
E'en spots no bigger than the husbandman's
Or shepherd's noontide dwarf-shrunk shadow spans
– Or e'en the milkmaid tripping through the dew,
Each space she covers with her slender shoe –
Seem to their view high woods in which they roam
As lorn, lost wanderers many miles from home,
Creeping up bents and down whole weary hours
And resting oft on the soft breasts of flowers;
Till age, in minutes long as years, creeps on,
Or waning summer warns them to be gone.

JOHN CLARE

The Fir-Tree

HANS CHRISTIAN ANDERSEN

Far down in the forest, where the warm sun and the fresh air made a sweet resting-place, grew a pretty little fir-tree; and yet it was not happy, it wished so much to be tall like its companions – the pines and firs which grew around it. The sun shone, and the soft air fluttered its leaves, and the little peasant children passed by, prattling merrily, but the fir-tree heeded them not. Sometimes the children would bring a large basket of raspberries or strawberries, wreathed on a straw, and seat themselves near the fir-tree, and say, 'Is it not a pretty little tree?' which made it feel more unhappy than before. And yet all this while the tree grew a notch or joint taller every year; for by the number of joints in the stem of a fir-tree we can discover its age. Still, as it grew, it complained, 'Oh! how I wish I were as tall as the other trees, then I would spread out my branches on every side, and my top would overlook the wide world. I should have the birds building their nests on my boughs, and when the wind blew, I should bow with stately dignity like my tall companions.' The tree was so discontented that it took no pleasure in the warm sunshine, the birds, or the rosy clouds that floated over it morning and evening. Sometimes, in winter, when the snow lay white and glittering on the ground, a hare would come springing along and jump right over the little tree; and then how mortified it would feel! Two winters passed, and when the third arrived, the tree had grown so tall that the hare was obliged to run round it. Yet it remained unsatisfied, and would exclaim, 'Oh, if I could but keep on growing tall and old! There is nothing else worth caring for in the world!' In the autumn, as usual, the woodcutters came and cut down several of the tallest trees, and the young fir-tree (which was now grown to its full height) shuddered as the noble trees fell to the earth with a crash. After the branches were lopped off, the trunks looked so slender and bare, that they could scarcely be recognized. Then they were placed upon wagons, and drawn by horses out of the forest. 'Where were they going? What would become of them?' The young fir-tree wished very much to know; so in the spring, when the swallows and the storks came, it asked, 'Do you know where those trees were taken? Did you meet them?'

The swallows knew nothing; but the stork, after a little reflection, nodded his head, and said, 'Yes, I think I do. I met several new ships when I flew from Egypt, and they had fine masts that smelt like fir. I think these must have been the trees; I assure you they were stately, very stately.'

'Oh, how I wish I were tall enough to go on the sea,' said the fir-tree. 'What is this sea, and what does it look like?'

'It would take too much time to explain,' said the stork, flying quickly away.

'Rejoice in thy youth,' said the sunbeam; 'rejoice in thy fresh growth, and the young life that is in thee.'

And the wind kissed the tree, and the dew watered it with tears; but the fir-tree regarded them not.

Christmas-time drew near, and many young trees were cut down, some even smaller and younger than the fir-tree who enjoyed neither rest nor peace with longing to leave its forest home. These young trees, which were chosen for their beauty, kept their branches, and were also laid on wagons and drawn by horses out of the forest.

'Where are they going?' asked the fir-tree. 'They are not taller than I am; indeed, one is much less; and why are the branches not cut off? Where are they going?'

'We know, we know,' sang the sparrows; 'we have looked in at the windows of the houses in the town, and we know what is done with them. They are dressed up in the most splendid manner. We have seen them standing in the middle of a warm room, and adorned with all sorts of beautiful things – honey cakes, gilded apples, playthings, and many hundreds of wax tapers.'

'And then,' asked the fir-tree, trembling through all its branches, 'and then what happens?'

'We did not see any more,' said the sparrows; 'but this was enough for us.'

'I wonder if anything so brilliant will ever happen to me,' thought the fir-tree. 'It would be much better than crossing the sea. I long for it almost with pain. Oh! when will Christmas be here? I am now as tall and well-grown as those which were taken away last year. Oh! that I were now laid on the wagon, or standing in the warm room, with all that brightness and splendour around me! Something better and more beautiful is to come after, or the trees would not be so decked out. Yes, what follows will be grander and more splendid. What can it be? I am weary with longing. I scarcely know how I feel.'

'Rejoice with us,' said the air and the sunlight. 'Enjoy thine own bright life in the fresh air.'

But the tree would not rejoice, though it grew taller every day; and, winter and summer, its dark-green foliage might be seen in the forest, while passers-by would say, 'What a beautiful tree!'

A short time before Christmas, the discontented fir-tree was the first to fall. As the axe cut through the stem, and

69

divided the pith, the tree fell with a groan to the earth, conscious of pain and faintness, and forgetting all its anticipations of happiness, in sorrow at leaving its home in the forest. It knew that it should never again see its dear old companions, the trees, nor the little bushes and many-coloured flowers that had grown by its side; perhaps not even the birds. Neither was the journey at all pleasant. The tree first recovered itself while being unpacked in the court-yard of a house, with several other trees; and it heard a man say, 'We only want one, and this is the prettiest.'

Then came two servants in grand livery, and carried the fir-tree into a large and beautiful apartment. On the walls hung pictures, and near the great stove stood great china vases, with lions on the lids. There were rocking-chairs, silken sofas, large tables covered with picture-books, and playthings, worth a great deal of money – at least, the children said so. Then the fir-tree was placed in a large tub, full of sand; but green baize hung all round it, so no one could see it was a tub, and it stood on a very handsome carpet. How the fir-tree trembled! 'What was going to happen to him now?' Some young ladies came, and helped them to adorn the tree. On one branch they hung little bags cut out of coloured paper, and each bag was filled with sweetmeats; from other branches hung gilded apples and walnuts, as if they had grown there; and above and all round were hundreds of red, blue and white tapers, which were fastened on the branches. Dolls, exactly like real babies, were placed under the green leaves, – the tree had never seen such things before, – and at the very top was fastened a glittering star, made of tinsel. Oh, it was very beautiful!

'This evening,' they all exclaimed, 'how bright it will be!' 'Oh, that the evening were come,' thought the tree, 'and the tapers lighted! then I shall know what else is going to happen. Will the trees of the forest come to see me? I wonder if the sparrows will peep in at the window as they fly? Shall I grow faster here, and keep on all these ornaments during summer and winter?' But guessing was of very little use; it made his bark ache, and this pain is as bad for a slender fir-tree, as headache is for us. At last the tapers were lighted, and then what a glistening blaze of light the tree presented! It trembled so with joy in all its branches, that one of the candles fell among the green leaves and burnt some of them. 'Help! help!' exclaimed the young ladies, but there was no danger, for they quickly extinguished the fire. After this, the tree tried not to tremble at all, though the fire frightened him; he was so anxious not to hurt any of the beautiful ornaments, even while their brilliancy dazzled him. And now the folding doors were thrown open, and a troop of children rushed in as if they intended to upset the tree; they were followed more slowly by their elders. For a moment the little ones stood silent with astonishment, and then they shouted for joy, till the room rang, and they danced merrily round the tree, while one present after another was taken from it.

'What are they doing? What will happen next?' thought the fir. At last the candles burnt down to the branches and were put out. Then the children received permission to plunder the tree.

Oh, how they rushed upon it, till the branches cracked, and had it not been fastened with the glistening star to the ceiling, it must have been thrown down. The children then danced about with their pretty toys, and no one noticed the tree, except the children's maid, who came and peeped among the branches to see if an apple or a fig had been forgotten.

'A story, a story,' cried the children, pulling a little fat man towards the tree.

'Now we shall be in the green shade,' said the man, as he seated himself under it, 'and the tree will have the pleasure of hearing also, but I shall only relate one story; what shall it be? Ivede-Avede, or Humpty Dumpty, who fell downstairs, but soon got up again, and at last married a princess.'

'Ivede-Avede,' cried some. 'Humpty Dumpty,' cried others, and there was a fine shouting and crying out. But the fir-tree remained quite still, and thought to himself, 'Shall I have anything to do with all this?' but he had already amused them as much as they wished. Then the old man told them the story of Humpty Dumpty, how he fell downstairs, and was raised up again, and married a princess. And the children clapped their hands and cried, 'Tell another, tell another,' for they wanted to hear the story of 'Ivede-Avede', but they had only had 'Humpty Dumpty'. After this the fir-tree became quite silent and thoughtful; never had the birds in the forest told such tales as 'Humpty Dumpty', who fell downstairs, and yet married a princess.

'Ah! yes, so it happens in the world,' thought the fir-tree; he believed it all, because it was related by such a nice man. 'Ah! well,' he thought, 'who knows? perhaps I may fall down, too, and marry a princess'; and he looked forward joyfully to the next evening, expecting to be again decked out with lights and playthings, gold and fruit. 'Tomorrow I will not tremble,' thought he; 'I will enjoy all my splendour, and I shall hear the story of Humpty Dumpty again, and perhaps Ivede-Avede.' And the tree remained quiet and thoughtful all night. In the morning the servants and the housemaid came in. 'Now,' thought the fir, 'all my splendour is going to begin again.' But they dragged him out of the room and upstairs to the garret, and threw him on the floor, in a dark corner, where no daylight shone, and there they left him. 'What does this mean?' thought the tree. 'What am I to do here? I can hear nothing in a place like this,' and he leant against the wall, and thought and thought. And he had time enough to think, for days and nights passed and no one came near him, and when at last somebody did come, it was only to put away large boxes in a corner. So the tree was completely hidden from sight as if it had never existed. 'It is winter now,' thought the tree, 'the ground is hard and covered with snow, so that people cannot plant me. I shall be sheltered here, I dare say, until spring comes. How thoughtful and kind everybody is to me! Still, I wish this place were not so dark, as well as lonely, with not even a little hare to look at. How pleasant it was out in the forest while the snow lay on the ground, when the hare would run by, yes, and jump over me, too, although I did not like it then. Oh! it is terribly lonely here.'

'Squeak, squeak,' said a little mouse, creeping cautiously towards the tree; then came another and they both sniffed at the fir-tree and crept between the branches.

'Oh, it is very cold,' said the little mouse, 'or else we should be so comfortable here, shouldn't we, you old fir-tree?'

'I am not old,' said the fir-tree, 'there are many who are older than I am.'

'Where do you come from? and what do you know?' asked the mice, who were full of curiosity. 'Have you seen the most beautiful places in the world, and can you tell us all about them? and have you been in the storeroom, where cheeses lie on the shelf, and hams hang from the ceiling? One can run about on tallow candles there, and go in thin and come out fat.'

'I know nothing of that place,' said the fir-tree, 'but I know the wood where the sun shines and the birds sing.' And then the tree told the little mice all about its youth. They had never heard such an account in their lives; and after they had listened to it attentively, they said, 'What a number of things you have seen! You must have been very happy.'

'Happy!' exclaimed the fir-tree, and then as he reflected upon what he had been telling them, he said, 'Ah, yes! after all, those were happy days.' But when he went on and related all about Christmas-eve, and how he had been dressed up with cakes and lights, the mice said, 'How happy you must have been, you old fir-tree.'

'I am not old at all,' replied the tree. 'I only came from the forest this winter, I am now checked in my growth.'

'What splendid stories you can relate,' said the little mice. And the next night four other mice came with them to hear what the tree had to tell. The more he talked, the more he remembered, and then he thought to himself, 'Those were happy days, but they may come again. Humpty Dumpty fell downstairs, and yet he married the princess; perhaps I may marry a princess, too.' And the fir-tree thought of a pretty little birch-tree that grew in the forest, which was to him a real beautiful princess.

'Who is Humpty Dumpty?' asked the little mice. And then the tree related the whole story; he could remember every single word, and the little mice were so delighted with it, that they were ready to jump to the top of the tree. The next night a great many more mice made their appearance, and on Sunday two rats came with them; but they said it was not a pretty story at all, and the little mice were very sorry, for it made them also think less of it.

'Do you know only one story?' asked the rats.

'Only one,' replied the fir-tree; 'I heard it on the happiest evening in my life; but I did not know I was so happy at the time.'

'We think it a very miserable story,' said the rats. 'Don't you know any story about bacon, or tallow in the storeroom?'

'No,' replied the tree.

'Many thanks to you, then,' replied the rats, and they marched off.

The little mice also kept away after this, and the tree sighed, and said, 'It was very pleasant when the merry little mice sat round me and listened while I talked. Now that is all past, too. However, I shall consider myself happy when someone comes to take me out of this place.' But would this ever happen? Yes; one morning people came to clear out the garret, and the tree was pulled out of the corner and thrown roughly on the garret floor; then the servant dragged it out upon the staircase where the daylight shone. 'Now life is beginning again,' said the tree, rejoicing in the sunshine and the fresh air. Then it was taken downstairs and out into the courtyard so quickly, that it forgot to think of itself, and could only look about, there was so much to be seen. The court was close to a garden, where everything looked blooming. Fresh and fragrant roses hung over the little palings. The linden trees were in blossom; while the swallows flew here and there, crying, 'Twit, twit, my mate is coming,' – but it was not the fir-tree they meant. 'Now I shall live,' cried the tree, joyfully spreading out its branches; but alas! they were all withered and yellow, and it lay in a corner amongst weeds and nettles. The star of gold paper still stuck in the top of the tree and glittered in the sunshine. In the same courtyard two of the merry children were playing who had danced round the tree at Christmas, and had been so happy. The youngest saw the gilded star, and ran and pulled it off the tree. 'Look what is sticking to the ugly old fir-tree,' said the child, treading on the branches till they crackled under his boots. And the tree saw all the fresh bright flowers in the garden, and then looked at itself, and wished it had

75

remained in the dark corner of the garret. It thought of its fresh youth in the forest, of the merry Christmas evening, and of the little mice who had listened to the story of 'Humpty Dumpty'. 'Past! past!' said the old tree; 'Oh, had I but enjoyed myself while I could have done so! but now it is too late.' Then a lad came and chopped the tree into small pieces, till a large bundle lay in a heap on the ground. The pieces were placed in a fire under the copper, and they quickly blazed up brightly while the tree sighed so deeply that each sigh was like a little pistol shot. Then the children, who were at play, came and seated themselves in front of the fire, and looked at it, and cried, 'Pop, pop.' But at each 'pop', which was a deep sigh, the tree was thinking of a summer day in the forest, or of some winter night there, when the stars shone brightly; and of Christmas evening, and of 'Humpty Dumpty', the only story it had ever heard or knew how to relate, till at last it was consumed. The boys still played in the garden, and the youngest wore the golden star on his breast, with which the tree had been adorned during the happiest evening of its existence. Now all was past; the tree's life was past, and the story also – for all stories must come to an end at last.

*

The Holly and the Ivy

The holly and the ivy,
When they are both full grown,
Of all the trees that are in the wood
The holly bears the crown.
> O the rising of the sun
> And the running of the deer,
> The playing of the merry organ,
> Sweet singing in the choir.

The holly bears a blossom
As white as the lily flower,
And Mary bore sweet Jesus Christ
To be our sweet saviour.

O the rising of the sun
And the running of the deer,
The playing of the merry organ,
Sweet singing in the choir.

The holly bears a berry
As red as any blood,
And Mary bore sweet Jesus Christ
To do poor sinners good.

O the rising of the sun
And the running of the deer,
The playing of the merry organ,
Sweet singing in the choir.

The holly bears a prickle
As sharp as any thorn,
And Mary bore swect Jesus Christ
On Christmas Day in the morn.

O the rising of the sun
And the running of the deer,
The playing of the merry organ,
Sweet singing in the choir,

The holly bears a bark
As bitter as any gall.
And Mary bore sweet Jesus Christ
For to redeem us all.

O the rising of the sun
And the running of the deer,
The playing of the merry organ,
Sweet singing in the choir.

TRADITIONAL

The Herball, or General Historie of Plants

JOHN GERARD

John Gerard was a horticulturist and had charge of Lord Burghley's gardens; he also practised as a barber-surgeon, so it is understandable that he was much concerned with the medicinal qualities of plants and trees. It is said that he stole much from an earlier work, but he must surely have had great personal experience of these matters. If some of his comments and remedies seem quaint to us now, it should be remembered that pharmacology still employs many extracts and tinctures known to Gerard, and that herbal medicine still flourishes.
John Gerard wrote his Herball *in 1597.*

*

Beech Tree

The Beech is an high tree, with boughes spreading often-times in manner of a circle, and with a thicke body having many armes: the bark is smooth; the timber is white, hard, and very profitable; the leaves be smooth, thin, broad, and lesser than those of the blacke Poplar: the catkins or blowings be also lesser and shorter than those of the Birch tree and yellow; the fruit or Mast is contained in a huske or cup that is prickly, and rough-bristled, yet not so much as that of the Chestnut: which fruit being taken forth of the shells or urchin huskes, be covered with a soft and smooth skin like in colour and smoothenesse to the Chestnuts, but they be much lesser, and of another forme, that is to say, triangled or three cornered; the kernell within is sweet, with a certain astriction or binding qualitie: the roots be few and grow not deepe, and little lower than under the turfe.

The Beech tree loveth a plaine and open country, and groweth very plentifully in many Forrests and desart places of Sussex, Kent and sundry other countries.

The Beech floureth in Aprill and May, and the fruit is

ripe in September, at what time the Deere do eat the same very greedily, as greatly delighting therein; which hath caused forresters and huntsmen to call it Buck-mast.

The leaves of Beech are very profitably applied unto hot swellings, blisters and excoriations; and being chewed they are good for chapped lips and paine of the gums.

The kernels or mast within are reported to ease the paine of the kidnies if they be eaten. With these, mice and squirrels are greatly delighted, who do mightily increase by feeding thereon: Swine also be fatned herewith, and certain other beasts: also Deere doe feed thereon very greedily: they be likewise pleasant to Thrushes and Pigeons.

Petrus Crescentius writeth, That the ashes of the wood is good to make glasse with.

The water that is found in the hollownesse of Beeches cureth the naughty scurfe, tetters and scabs of men, horses, kine and sheepe, if they be washed therewith.

Birch Tree

The common Birch tree waxeth likewise a great tree, having many boughs beset with small rods or twigs, very limber and pliant; the barke of the yong twigs and branches is plain, smooth, and full of sap, in colour like the chestnut, but the rind of the body or trunk is hard without, white, rough, and uneven, full of chinks or crevises: under which is found another fine barke, plaine, smooth, and as thin as paper, which heretofore was used in stead of paper to write on, before the making of paper was known: in Russia and these cold countries it served in stead of tiles and slate to cover their houses withall. This tree beareth for his flours certain aglets like the Hasel tree, but smaller, wherein the seed is contained.

The common Birch tree grows in woods, fenny grounds, and mountains, in most places of England.

The catkins or aglets do first appear, and then the leaves, in Aprill or a little later.

Concerning the medicinable use of the Birch tree, or his parts, there is nothing extant either in the old or new writers.

This tree, saith *Pliny, lib. 16, cap. 18, Mirabili candore & tenuitate terribilis magistratuum virgis*: for in times past the magistrates rods were made thereof; and in our time also Schoolmasters and Parents do terrifie their children with rods made of Birch . . .

Corne

This kinde of Wheate is the most principall of all other whose eares are altogether bare or naked, without awnies or chaffie beards. The stalke riseth from a threddy root, compact of many strings, joynted or kneed at sundry distances; from whence shoot forth grassie blades and leaves like unto Rie, but broader. The plant is so well known to many, and so profitable to all, that the meanest and most ignorant need no larger description to know the same by.

Wheat (saith *Galen*) is very much used of men, and with greatest profit. Those Wheats do nourish most that be hard, and have their whole substance so closely compact as they can scarsely be bit asunder; for such do nourish very much: and the contrary but little.

Slices of fine white bread laid to infuse or steepe in Rose water, and so applied unto sore eyes which have many hot humours falling into them, doe easily defend the humour, and cease the paine.

The oyle of wheat pressed forth betweene two plates of hot iron, healeth the chaps and chinks of the hands, feet, and fundament, which come of cold, making smooth the hands, face or any other part of the body.

Corn-Rose or *Wilde Poppy*

The stalks of red Poppy be blacke, tender and brittle, some-what hairy; the leaves are cut round about like those of Succorie or Wild Rocket. The flours grow forth at the tops of the stalks, being of a beautifull and gallant red colour, with blackish threds compassing about the middle part of the head, which being fully growne, is lesser than that of the garden Poppy: the seed is small and blacke . . .

Most men being led rather by false experiments than reason, commend the flours against the Pleurisie, giving to drink as soon as the pain comes, either the distilled water, or syrup made by often infusing the leaves. And yet many times it happens, that the paine ceaseth by that meanes . . .

THE SEASONS

The Last Snow

Although the snow still lingers
Heaped on the ivy's blunt webbed fingers
And painting tree-trunks on one side,
Here in this sunlit ride
The fresh unchristened things appear;
Leaf, spathe and stem,
With crumbs of earth clinging to them
To show the way they came
But no flower yet to tell their name,
And one green spear
Stabbing a dead leaf from below
Kills winter at a blow.

ANDREW YOUNG

First Sight

Lambs that learn to walk in snow
When their bleating clouds the air
Meet a vast unwelcome, know
Nothing but a sunless glare.
Newly stumbling to and fro
All they find, outside the fold
Is a wretched width of cold.

As they wait beside the ewe,
Her fleeces wetly caked, there lies
Hidden round them, waiting too,
Earth's immeasurable surprise.
They could not grasp it if they knew,
What so soon will wake and grow
Utterly unlike the snow.

PHILIP LARKIN

The Year's Awakening

How do you know that the pilgrim track
Along the belting zodiac
Swept by the sun in his seeming rounds
Is traced by now to the Fishes' bounds
And into the Ram, when weeks of cloud
Have wrapt the sky in a clammy shroud,
And never as yet a tinct of spring
Has shown in the Earth's apparelling;
   O vespering bird, how do you know,
     How do you know?

How do you know, deep underground,
Hid in your bed from sight and sound,
Without a turn in temperature,
With weather life can scarce endure,
That light has won a fraction's strength,
And day put on some moments' length,
Whereof in merest rote will come,
Weeks hence, mild airs that do not numb;
   O crocus root, how do you know,
     How do you know?

THOMAS HARDY

Twixt Martinmas and Yule
Water's worth wine in any pool.

He who in January sows oats —
Gets gold and groats.

Written in Early Spring

I heard a thousand blended notes
 While in a grove I sat reclined,
In that sweet mood when pleasant thoughts
 Bring sad thoughts to the mind.

To her fair work did Nature link
 The human soul that through me ran;
And much it grieved my heart to think
 What man has made of man.

Through primrose tufts, in that green bower,
 The periwinkle trail'd its wreaths;
And 'tis my faith that every flower
 Enjoys the air it breathes.

The birds around me hopp'd and play'd,
  Their thoughts I cannot measure –
But the least motion that they made
  It seem'd a thrill of pleasure.

The budding twigs spread out their fan
  To catch the breezy air;
And I must think, do all I can,
  That there was pleasure there.

If this belief from heaven be sent,
  If such be Nature's holy plan,
Have I not reason to lament
  What man has made of man?

WILLIAM WORDSWORTH

The cuckoo sings in April,
The cuckoo sings in May,
The cuckoo sings at Midsummer –
But not upon the Day.

Spring

The sweet season that bud and bloom forth brings,
With green hath clad the hill and eke the vale;
The nightingale with feathers new she sings;
The turtle to her mate hath told her tale.
Summer is come, for every spray now springs,
The hart hath hung his old head on the pale;
The buck in brake his winter coat now flings,
The fishes float with new repaired scale;
The adder all her slough away she flings,
The swift swallow pursue the flies small.
The busy bee her honey now she mings;
Winter is worn that was the flowers' bale.
And thus I see, among these pleasant things,
Each care decays, and yet my sorrow springs.

HENRY HOWARD, EARL OF SURREY

The First Primrose

MARY RUSSELL MITFORD

Mary Russell Mitford, the author of Our Village, *from which this extract is taken, was born in 1757. Her father was a doctor, extravagant to the point of madness, a born gambler. He took his young daughter, on her tenth birthday, to buy an unusual present – a lottery ticket. It must have seemed rather a dismal thing, to have only a bit of paper in her hand to celebrate the day. However, that ticket won Mary the enormous sum of £20,000 – and it really was an enormous sum in those days. This paid for an education that her father would never have felt himself able to give her – though he ran through several fortunes and the remains of the twenty thousand, before dying in monstrous debt and leaving poor Mary penniless. Happily she had many friends and was already known as a writer, so there was help at hand, and very shortly she was awarded a pension from the Crown. These hard facts make a curious background to the spirit and freshness of her writing – sentimental, eager, yet never false, and full of an intense love of the countryside.*

*

March 6th. – Fine March weather: boisterous, blustering, much wind and squalls of rain; and yet the sky, where the clouds are swept away, deliciously blue, with snatches of sunshine, bright, and clear, and healthful, and the roads, in spite of the slight glittering showers, crisply dry. Altogether the day is tempting, very tempting. It will not do for the dear common, that windmill of a walk; but the close sheltered lanes at the bottom of the hill, which keep out just enough of the stormy air, and let in all the sun, will be delightful. Past our old house, and round by the winding lanes, and the workhouse, and across the lea, and so into the turnpike-road again, – that is our route for today. Forth we set, Mayflower and I, rejoicing in the sunshine, and still more in the wind, which gives such an intense feeling of existence, and, co-operating with brisk motion, sets our blood and our spirits in a glow. For mere physical pleasure, there is nothing perhaps equal to the enjoyment of being drawn, in a light carriage, against such a wind as this, by a blood-horse at his height of speed. Walking comes next to it; but walking is not quite so luxurious or so spiritual, not quite so much what one fancies of flying, or being carried above the clouds in a balloon.

Nevertheless, a walk is a good thing; especially under this southern hedgerow, where nature is just beginning to live again; the periwinkles, with their starry blue flowers, and their shining myrtle-like leaves, garlanding the bushes; woodbines and elder-trees pushing out their small swelling buds; and grasses and mosses springing forth in every variety of brown and green. Here we are at the corner where four lanes meet, or rather where a passable road of stones and gravel crosses an impassable one of beautiful but treacherous turf, and where the small white farmhouse, scarcely larger than a cottage, and the well-stocked rick-yard behind, tell of comfort and order, but leave all unguessed the great riches of the master. How he became so rich is almost a puzzle; for, though the farm be his own, it is not large; and though prudent and frugal on ordinary occasions, Farmer Barnard is no miser. His horses, dogs, and pigs are the best kept in the parish – May herself, although her beauty be injured by her fatness, half envies the plight of his bitch Fly: his wife's gowns and shawls cost as much again as any shawls in the village; his dinner parties (to be sure they are not frequent) display twice the ordinary quantity of good things – two couples of ducks, two dishes of green peas, two turkey poults, two gammons of bacon, two plum-puddings; moreover, he keeps a single-horse chaise, and has built and endowed a Methodist chapel. Yet is he the richest man in these parts. Everything prospers with him. Money drifts about him like snow. He looks like a rich man. There is a sturdy squareness of face and figure; a good-humoured obstinacy; a civil importance. He never boasts of his wealth, or gives himself undue airs; but nobody can meet him at market or vestry without finding out immediately that he is the richest man there. They have no child to all this money; but there is an adopted nephew, a fine spirited lad, who may, perhaps, some day or other, play the part of a fountain to the reservoir.

Now turn up the wide road till we come to the open common, with its park-like trees, its beautiful stream, wandering and twisting along, and its rural bridge. Here we turn again, past that other white farmhouse, half-hidden by the magnificent elms which stand before it. Ah! riches dwell not there, but there is found the next best thing – an industrious and light-hearted poverty. Twenty years ago Rachel Hilton was the prettiest and merriest lass in the country. Her father, an old gamekeeper, had retired to a village ale-house, where his good beer, his social humour, and his black-eyed daughter, brought much custom. She had lovers by the score; but Joseph White, the dashing and lively son of an opulent farmer, carried off the fair Rachel. They married and settled here, and here they live still, as merrily as ever, with fourteen

children of all ages and sizes, from nineteen years to nineteen months, working harder than any people in the parish, and enjoying themselves more. I would match them for labour and laughter against any family in England. She is a blithe, jolly dame, whose beauty has amplified into comeliness; he is tall, and thin, and bony, with sinews like a whipcord, a strong lively voice, a sharp weather-beaten face, and eyes and lips that smile and brighten when he speaks into a most contagious hilarity. They are very poor, and I often wish them richer; but I don't know – perhaps it might put them out.

Quite close to Farmer White's is a little ruinous cottage, white-washed once, and now in a sad state of betweenity, where dangling stockings and shirts, swelled by the wind, drying in a neglected garden, give signal of a washerwoman. There dwells, at present in single blessedness, Betty Adams, the wife of our sometimes gardener. I never saw anyone who so much reminded me in person of that lady whom everybody knows, Mistress Meg Merrilies – as tall, as grizzled, as stately, as dark, as gipsy-looking, bonneted and gowned like her prototype, and almost as oracular. Here the resemblance ceases. Mrs Adams is a perfectly honest, industrious, painstaking person, who earns a good deal of money by washing and charing, and spends it in other luxuries than tidiness – in green tea, and gin, and snuff. Her husband lives in a great family, ten miles off. He is a capital gardener – or rather he would be so, if he were not too ambitious. He undertakes all things, and finishes none. But a smooth tongue, a knowing look, and a great capacity of labour, carry him through. Let him but like his ale and his master, and he will do enough work for four. Give him his own way, and his full quantum, and nothing comes amiss to him.

Ah, May is bounding forward! Her silly heart leaps at the sight of the old place – and so in good truth does mine. What a pretty place it was – or rather how pretty I thought it! I suppose I should have thought any place so where I had spent eighteen happy years. But it was really pretty. A large, heavy, white house, in the simplest style, surrounded by fine oaks and elms, and tall massy plantations shaded down into a beautiful lawn by wild overgrown shrubs, bowery acacias, ragged sweet-briers, promontories of dogwood, and Portugal laurel, and bays, overhung by laburnum and bird-cherry; a long piece of water letting light into the picture, and looking just like a natural stream, the banks as rude and wild as the shrubbery, interspersed with broom, and furze, and bramble, and pollard oaks covered with ivy and honeysuckle; the whole enclosed by an old mossy park paling, and terminating in a series of rich meadows, richly planted. This is an exact description of the home which, three years ago, it nearly broke my heart to leave. What a tearing up by the root it was! I have pitied cabbage-plants and celery, and all transplantable things, ever since; though, in common with them, and with other vegetables, the first agony of the transportation being over, I have taken such firm and tenacious hold of my new soil, that I would not for the world be pulled up again, even to be restored to the old beloved ground – not even if its beauty were undiminished, which is by no means the case; for in those three years it has thrice changed masters, and every successive possessor has brought the curse of improvement upon the place; so that between filling up the water to cure dampness, cutting down trees to let in prospects, planting to keep them out, shutting up windows to darken the inside of the house (by which means one end looks precisely as an eight of spades would do that should have the misfortune to lose one of his corner pips), and building colonnades to lighten the out, added to a general clearance of pollards, and brambles, and ivy, and honeysuckles, and park palings, and irregular shrubs, the poor place is so transmogrified, that if it had its old looking-glass, the water, back again, it would not know its own face. And yet I love to haunt around about it: so does May. Her particular attraction is a certain broken bank full of rabbit burrows, into which she insinuates her long pliant head and neck, and tears her pretty feet by vain scratchings: mine is a warm sunny hedgerow, in the same remote field, famous for early flowers. Never was a spot more variously flowery: primrose yellow, lilac white, violets of either hue, cowslips, oxslips, arums, orchises, wild hyacinths, ground ivy, pansies, strawberries, heartsease, formed a small part of the Flora of that wild hedgerow. How profusely they covered the sunny open slope under the weeping birch, 'the lady of the woods' – and how often have I started to see the early innocent brown snake, who loved the spot as well as I did, winding along the young blossoms, or rustling amongst the fallen leaves! There are primrose leaves already, and short green buds, but no flowers; not even in that furze cradle so full of roots, where they used to blow as in a basket. No, my May, no rabbits! no primroses! We may as well get over the gate into the woody winding lane, which will bring us home again.

Here we are making the best of our way between the old elms that arch so solemnly overhead, dark and sheltered even now. They say that a spirit haunts this deep pool – a white lady without a head. I cannot say that I have seen her, often as I have paced this lane deep at midnight, to hear the nightingales or glow-worms – but there, better and rarer than a thousand ghosts, dearer even than nightingales or

glow-worms, there is a primrose, the first of the year; a tuft of primroses, springing in yonder sheltered nook, from the mossy roots of an old willow, and living again in the clear bright pool. Oh, how beautiful they are – three fully blown, and two bursting buds! How glad I am I came this way! They are not to be reached. Even Jack Rapley's love of the difficult and the unattainable would fail him here: May herself could not stand on that steep bank. So much the better. Who would wish to disturb them? There they live in their innocent and fragrant beauty, sheltered from the storms, and rejoicing in the sunshine, and looking as if they could feel their happiness. Who would wish to disturb them? Oh, how glad I am I came this way home!

(from *Our Village*)

*

May

I cannot tell you how it was:
But this I know: it came to pass
Upon a bright and breezy day
When May was young; ah pleasant May!
As yet the poppies were not born
Between the blades of tender corn;
The last eggs were not hatched as yet.
Nor any bird forgone its mate.

I cannot tell you how it was;
But this I know: it came to pass.
It passed away with sunny May,
With all sweet things it passed away,
And left me old, and cold, and grey.

CHRISTINA ROSSETTI

May Day

FLORA THOMPSON

After the excitement of the concert came the long winter months, when snowstorms left patches on the ploughed fields, like scrapings of sauce on left-over pieces of Christmas pudding, until the rains came and washed them away and the children, carrying old umbrellas to school, had them turned inside out by the wind, and cottage chimneys smoked and washing had to be dried indoors. But at last came spring and spring brought May Day, the greatest day in the year from the children's point of view.

The May garland was all that survived there of the old May Day festivities. The maypole and the May games and May dances in which whole parishes had joined had long been forgotten. Beyond giving flowers for the garland and pointing out how things should be done and telling how they had been done in their own young days, the older people took no part in the revels.

For the children as the day approached all hardships were forgotten and troubles melted away. The only thing that mattered was the weather. 'Will it be fine?' was the constant question, and many an aged eye was turned skyward in response to read the signs of wind and cloud. Fortunately, it was always reasonably fine. Showers there were, of course, at that season, but never a May Day of hopelessly drenching rain, and the May garland was carried in procession every year throughout the eighties.

The garland was made, or 'dressed', in the school-room. Formerly it had been dressed out of doors, or in one of the cottages, or in someone's barn; but dressed it had been and probably in much the same fashion for countless generations.

The foundation of the garland was a light wooden framework of uprights supporting graduated hoops, forming a bell-shaped structure about four feet high. This frame was covered with flowers, bunched and set closely, after the manner of wreath-making.

On the last morning of April the children would come to school with bunches, baskets, arms and pinafores full of flowers – every blossom they could find in the fields and hedges or beg from parents and neighbours. On the previous Sunday some of the bigger boys would have walked six or eight miles to a distant wood where primroses grew. These, with violets from the hedgerows, cowslips from the meadows, and wallflowers, oxlips, and sprays of pale red flowering currant from the cottage gardens formed the main supply. A sweetbriar hedge in the schoolmistress's garden furnished unlimited greenery.

Piled on desks, table, and floor, this supply appeared inexhaustible; but the garland was large, and as the work of dressing it proceeded, it soon became plain that the present stock wouldn't 'hardly go nowheres', as the children said. So foraging parties were sent out, one to the Rectory, another to Squire's, and others to outlying farmhouses and cottages. All returned loaded, for even the most miserly and garden-proud gave liberally to the garland. In time the wooden frame was covered, even if there had to be solid greenery to fill up at the back, out of sight. Then the 'Top-knot', consisting of a bunch of crown imperial, yellow and brown, was added to crown the whole, and the fragrant, bowering structure was sprinkled with water and set aside for the night.

While the garland was being dressed, an older girl, perhaps the May Queen herself, would be busy in a corner making the crown. This always had to be a daisy crown; but, meadow daisies being considered too common, and also possessing insufficient staying power, garden daisies, white and red, were used, with a background of dark, glossy, evergreen leaves.

The May Queen had been chosen weeks beforehand. She was supposed to be either the prettiest or the most popular girl in the parish; but it was more often a case of self-election by the strongest willed or of taking turns: 'You choose me this year and I'll choose you next.' However elected, the queens had a strong resemblance to each other, being stout-limbed, rosy-cheeked maidens of ten or eleven, with great manes of dark hair frizzed out to support the crown becomingly.

95

The final touches were given the garland when the children assembled at six o'clock on May Day morning. Then a large china doll in a blue frock was brought forth from the depths of the school needlework chest and arranged in a sitting position on a little ledge in the centre front of the garland. This doll was known as 'the lady', and a doll of some kind was considered essential. Even in those parishes where the garland had degenerated into a shabby nosegay carried aloft at the top of a stick, some dollish image was mixed in with the flowers. The attitude of the children to the lady is interesting. It was understood that the garland was her garland, carried in her honour. The lady must never be roughly handled. If the garland turned turtle, as it was apt to do later in the day, when the road was rough and the bearers were growing weary, the first question was always, 'Is the lady all right?' (Is it possible that the lady was once 'Our Lady', she having in her turn, perhaps, replaced an earlier effigy of some pagan spirit of the newly decked earth?)

The lady comfortably settled in front of the garland, a large white muslin veil or skirt, obviously borrowed from a Victorian dressing-table, was draped over the whole to act as drop-scene and sunshade combined. Then a broomstick was inserted between the hoops for carrying purposes.

All the children in the parish between the ages of seven and eleven were by this time assembled, those girls who possessed them wearing white or light coloured frocks, irrespective of the temperature, and girls and boys alike decked out with bright ribbon knots and bows and sashes, those of the boys worn crosswise over one shoulder. The queen wore her daisy crown with a white veil thrown over it, and the other girls who could procure them also wore white veils. White gloves were traditional, but could seldom be obtained. A pair would sometimes be found for the queen, always many sizes too large; but the empty finger-ends came in handy to suck in a bashful mood when, later on, the kissing began.

The procession then formed. It was as follows:

Boy with flag.   Girl with money box.
           THE GARLAND with two bearers.
                King and queen.

96

Two maids of honour.
Lord and Lady.
Two maids of honour.
Footman and footman's lady.
Rank and file, walking in twos.

Girl known as 'Mother'.   Boy called 'Ragman'.

The 'Mother' was one of the most dependable of the older girls who was made responsible for the behaviour of the garlanders. She carried a large, old-fashioned, double-lidded marketing basket over her arm, containing the lunches of the principal actors. The boy called 'Ragman' carried the coats brought in case of rain, but seldom worn, even during a shower, lest by their poverty and shabbiness thay should disgrace the festive attire.

The procession stepped out briskly. Mothers waved and implored their offspring to behave well; some of the little ones left behind lifted up their voices and wept; old people came to cottage gates and said that, though well enough, this year's procession was poor compared to some they had seen. But the garlanders paid no heed; they had their feet on the road at last and vowed they would not turn back now, 'not if it rained cats and dogs'.

The first stop was at the Rectory, where the garland was planted before the front door and the shrill little voices struck up, shyly at first, but gathering confidence as they went on:

> A bunch of may I have brought you
>   And at your door it stands.
> It is but a sprout, but it's well put about
>   By the Lord Almighty's hands.
>
> God bless the master of this house
>   God bless the mistress too,
> And all the little children
>   That round the table go.
>
> And now I've sung my short little song
>   I must no longer stay.
> God bless you all, both great and small,
>   And send you a happy May Day.

During the singing of this the Rector's face, wearing its mildest expression, and bedaubed with shaving lather, for it was only as yet seven o'clock, would appear at an upper window and nod approval and admiration of the garland. His daughter would be down and at the door, and for her the veil was lifted and the glory of the garland revealed. She would look, touch and smell, then slip a silver coin into the money-box, and the procession would move on towards Squire's.

There, the lady of the house would bow haughty approval and if there were visiting grandchildren the lady would be detached from the garland and held up to their nursery window to be admired. Then Squire himself would appear in the stable doorway with a brace of sniffing, suspicious spaniels at his heels. 'How many are there of you?' he would call. 'Twenty-seven? Well, here's a five-bob bit for you. Don't quarrel over it. Now let's have a song.'

'Not "A Bunch of May",' the girl called Mother would whisper, impressed by the five-shilling piece; 'not that old-fashioned thing. Something newer,' and something newer, though still not very new, would be selected. Perhaps it would be:

> All hail gentle spring
>   With thy sunshine and showers,
> And welcome the sweet buds
>   That burst in the bowers;
> Again we rejoice as thy light step and free
> Brings leaves to the woodland and flowers to the bee,
> Bounding, bounding, bounding, bounding,
>   Joyful and gay,
> Light and airy, like a fairy
>   Come, come away.

Or it might be:

> Come see our new garland, so green and so gay;
> 'Tis the firstfruits of spring and the glory of May.
> Here are cowslips and daisies and hyacinths blue,
> Here are buttercups bright and anemones too.

During the singing of the latter song, as each flower was mentioned, a specimen bloom would be pointed to in the gar-

land. It was always a point of honour to have at least one of each named in the several verses; though the hawthorn was always a difficulty, for in the south midlands May's own flower seldom opens before the middle of that month. However, there was always at least one knot of tight green flower buds.

After becoming duty had been paid to the Rectory and Big House, the farmhouse and cottages were visited; then the little procession set out along narrow, winding country roads, with tall hedges of blackthorn and bursting leaf-buds on either side, to make its seven-mile circuit. In those days there were no motors to dodge and there was very little other traffic; just a farm cart here and there, or the baker's white-tilted van, or a governess car with nurses and children out for their airing. Sometimes the garlanders would forsake the road for stiles and footpaths across buttercup meadows, or go through parks and gardens to call at some big house or secluded farmstead.

In the ordinary course, country children of that day seldom went beyond their own parish bounds, and this long trek opened up new country to most of them. There was a delightful element of exploration about it. New short cuts would be tried, one year through a wood, another past the fishponds, or across such and such a paddock, where there might, or might not, be a bull. On one pond they passed sailed a solitary swan; on the terrace before one mansion peacocks spread their tails in the sun; the ram which pumped the water to one house mystified them with its subterranean thudding. There were often showers, and to Laura, looking back after fifty years, the whole scene would melt into a blur of wet greenery, with rainbows and cuckoo-calls and, overpowering all other impressions, the wet wallflower and primrose scent of the May garland.

Sometimes on the road a similar procession from another village came into view; but never one with so magnificent a garland. Some of them, indeed, had nothing worth calling a garland at all; only nosegays tied mopwise on sticks. No lord and lady, no king and queen; only a rabble begging with money-boxes. Were the Fordlow and Lark Rise folks sorry

for them? No. They stuck out their tongues, and, forgetting
their pretty May songs, yelled:

> Old Hardwick skags!
> Come to Fordlow to pick up rags
> To mend their mothers' pudding-bags,
> Yah! Yah!

and the rival troop retaliated in the same strain.

At the front door calls, the queen and her retinue stood
demurely behind the garland and helped with the singing,
unless Her Majesty was called forward to have her crown in-
spected and admired. It was at the back doors of large houses
that the fun began. In the country houses at that date troops
of servants were kept, and the May Day procession would
find the courtyard crowded with house-maids and kitchen-
maids, dairy-maids and laundry-maids, footmen, grooms,
coachmen, and gardeners. The songs were sung, the garland
was admired; then, to a chorus of laughter, teasing and
urging, one Maid of Honour snatched the cap from the King's
head, the other raised the Queen's veil, and a shy, sheepish
boy pecked at his companion's rosy cheek, to the huge delight
of the beholders.

'Again! Again!' a dozen voices would cry and the kissing
was repeated until the royal couple turned sulky and refused
to kiss any more, even when offered a penny a kiss. Then the
lord saluted his lady and the footman the footman's lady (this
couple had probably been introduced in compliment to such
patrons), and the money-box was handed round and began to
grow heavy with pence.

The menservants, with their respectable side-whiskers, the
maids in their little flat caps like crocheted mats on their
smoothly parted hair, and their long, billowing lilac or pink
print gowns, and the children in their ribbon-decked poverty,
alike belong to a bygone order of things. The boys pulled
forelocks and the girls dropped curtseys to the upper servants
for they came next in importance to 'the gentry'. Some of
them really belonged to a class which would not be found in
service today; for at that time there was little hospital nursing,
teaching, typing, or shop work to engage the daughters of

small farmers, small shopkeepers, innkeepers and farm bailiffs. Most of them had either to go out to service or remain at home.

After the mansion, there were the steward's, the head gardener's and the stud-groom's houses to visit with the garland; then on through gardens and park and woods and fields to the next stopping-place. Things did not always go smoothly. Feet got tired, especially when boots did not fit properly or were worn thin. Squabbles broke out among the boys and sometimes had to be settled by a fight. Often a heavy shower would send the whole party packing under trees for shelter, with the unveiled garland freshening outside in the rain; or some irate gamekeeper would turn the procession back from a short cut, adding miles to the way. But these were slight drawbacks to happiness on a day as near to perfection as anything can be in human life.

There came a point in the circuit when faces were turned towards home, instead of away from it; and at last, at long last, the lights in the Lark Hill windows shone clear through the spring twilight. The great day was over, for ever, as it seemed, for at ten years old a year seems as long as a century. Still, there was the May money to be shared out in school the next morning, and the lady to be stroked before being put back in her box, and the flowers which had survived to be put in water: even tomorrow would not be quite a common day. So the last waking thoughts blended with dreams of swans and peacocks and footmen and sore feet and fat cooks with pink faces wearing daisy crowns which turned into pure gold, then melted away.

(from *Lark Rise to Candleford*, 1939)

The fair maid who, the first of May,
Goes to the fields at break of day
And washes in dew from the hawthorn tree,
Will ever after handsome be.

The Rainy Summer

There's much afoot in heaven and earth this year;
   The winds hunt up the sun, hunt up the moon,
Trouble the dubious dawn, hasten the drear
   Height of a threatening noon.

No breath of boughs, no breath of leaves, of fronds,
   May linger or grow warm; the trees are loud;
The forest, rooted, tosses in her bonds,
   And strains against the cloud.

No scents may pause within the garden-fold;
   The rifled flowers are cold as ocean-shells;
Bees, humming in the storm, carry their cold
   Wild honey to cold cells.

ALICE MEYNELL

Sheep-Shearing Song

Come all my jolly boys and we'll together go,
Together with our masters to shear the lambs and 'yowes'.
All in the month of June of all times in the year
It always comes in season the lambs and 'yowes' to shear.
And then we will work hard, my boys, until our backs do
    break,
Our Master he will bring us beer whenever we do lack.

Our Master he comes round to see our work's done well,
And he says, Shear them close, my boys, for there is but little
    wool,
O, yes, good Master, we reply, we'll do as well as we can.
Our Captain cries, Shear close, my lads, to each and every
    man,
And at some places still we have this story all day long,
Bend your backs and shear them well, and this is all their
    song.

And then our noble Captain doth to the Master say,
Come let us have one bucket of your good ale, I pray,
He turns unto our Captain and makes him this reply,
You shall have the best of beer, I promise, presently.
Then with the foaming bucket pretty Betsy she doth come
And Master says, Maid, mind and see that every man has
    some.

This is some of our pastime while we the sheep do shear,
And though we are such merry boys, we work hard, I
    declare,
And when 'tis night and we are done our Master is more
    free
And stores us well with good strong beer and pipes of
    tobaccee,
And there we sit a-drinking we smoke and sing and roar,
Till we become far merrier than e'er we were before.

When all our work is done and all the sheep are shorn
Then home with our Captain to drink the ale that's strong.
It's a barrel then of hum-cap which we will call Black Ram,
And we do sit and swagger and we swear that we are men.
And yet before the night is through I'll bet you half-a-
crown,
That if you ha'n't a special care that Ram will knock you
down.

JIM COPPER

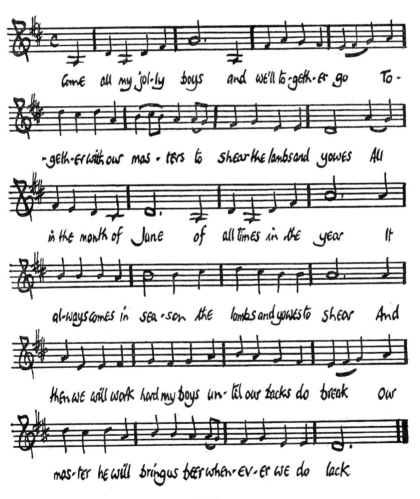

Come all my jolly boys and we'll together go To-
-gether with our masters to shear the lambs and yowes All
in the month of June of all times in the year It
always comes in season the lambs and yowes to shear And
then we will work hard my boys until our backs do break Our
master he will bring us beer whenever we do lack.

The Rain

I hear leaves drinking rain;
  I hear rich leaves on top
Giving the poor beneath
  Drop after drop;
'Tis a sweet noise to hear
These green leaves drinking near.

And when the Sun comes out,
  After this rain shall stop,
A wondrous light will fill
  Each dark, round drop;
I hope the Sun shines bright;
'Twill be a lovely sight.

W. H. DAVIES

A dry May and a rainy June
Puts the farmer's pipe in tune.

St Swithin's Day if thou dost rain
For forty days it will remain.

Oak before ash, summer will splash;
Ash before oak – summer will soak.

Blackberry-Picking

For Philip Hobsbaum

Late August, given heavy rain and sun
For a full week, the blackberries would ripen.
At first, just one, a glossy purple clot
Among others, red, green, hard as a knot.
You ate that first one and its flesh was sweet
Like thickened wine: summer's blood was in it
Leaving stains upon the tongue and lust for
Picking. Then red ones inked up and that hunger
Sent us out with milk-cans, pea-tins, jam-pots
Where briars scratched and wet grass bleached our boots.
Round hayfields, cornfields and potato-drills
We trekked and picked until the cans were full,
Until the tinkling bottom had been covered
With green ones, and on top big dark blobs burned
Like a plate of eyes. Our hands were peppered
With thorn pricks, our palms sticky as Bluebeard's.

We hoarded the fresh berries in the byre.
But when the bath was filled we found a fur,
A rat-grey fungus, glutting on our cache.
The juice was stinking too. Once off the bush
The fruit fermented, the sweet flesh would turn sour.
I always felt like crying. It wasn't fair
That all the lovely canfuls smelt of rot.
Each year I hoped they'd keep, knew they would not.

SEAMUS HEANEY

Hop-Picking

GEORGE ORWELL

One day at hop-picking was very much like another. At about a quarter to six in the morning we crawled out of the straw, put on our coats and boots (we slept in everything else) and went out to get a fire going – rather a job this September, when it rained all the time. By half past six we had made tea and fried some bread for breakfast, and then we started off for work, with bacon sandwiches and a drum of cold tea for our dinner. If it didn't rain we were working pretty steadily till about one, and then we would start a fire between the vines, heat up our tea and knock off for half an hour. After that we were at it again till half past five, and by the time we had got home, cleaned the hop-juice off our hands and had tea, it was already dark and we were dropping with sleep. A good many nights, though, we used to go out and steal apples. There was a big orchard near by, and three or four of us used to rob it systematically, carrying a sack and getting half a hundredweight of apples at a time, besides several pounds of cobnuts. On Sundays we used to wash our shirts and socks in the stream, and sleep the rest of the day. As far as I remember I never undressed completely all the time we were down there, nor washed my teeth, and I only shaved twice a week. Between working and getting meals (and that meant fetching everlasting cans of water, struggling with wet faggots, frying in tin-lids, etc.) one seemed to have not an instant to spare. I only read one book all the time I was down there, and that was a Buffalo Bill. Counting up what we spent I find that Ginger and I fed ourselves on about 5s. a week each, so it is not surprising that we were constantly short of tobacco and constantly hungry, in spite of the apples and what the others gave us. We seemed to be forever doing sums in farthings to find out whether we could afford another half ounce of shag or another two-pennorth of bacon. It wasn't a bad life, but what with standing all day, sleeping rough and getting my hands cut to bits, I felt a wreck at the end of it. It was humiliating to see that most of the people there looked on it as a holiday – in fact, it is because hopping is regarded as a holiday that the pickers will take such starvation wages. It gives one an insight into the lives of farm labourers, too, to realize that according to their standards hop-picking is hardly work at all.

One night a youth knocked at our door and said that he was a new picker and had been told to sleep in our hut. We let him in and fed him in the morning, after which he vanished. It appeared that he was not a picker at all, but a tramp, and that tramps often work this dodge in the hopping season, in order to get a kip under shelter. Another night a woman who was going home asked me to help her get her luggage to Wateringbury station. As she was leaving early they had paid her

off at eight bushels a shilling, and her total earnings were only just enough to get herself and family home. I had to push a perambulator, with one eccentric wheel and loaded with huge packages, two and a half miles through the dark, followed by a retinue of yelling children. When we got to the station the last train was just coming in, and in rushing the pram across the level crossing I upset it. I shall never forget that moment – the train bearing down on us, and the porter and I chasing a tin chamberpot that was rolling up the track. On several nights Ginger tried to persuade me to come and rob the church with him, and he would have done it alone if I had not managed to get it into his head that suspicion was bound to fall on him, as a known criminal. He had robbed churches before, and he said, what surprised me, that there is generally something worth having in the Poor-box. We had one or two jolly nights, on Saturdays, sitting round a huge fire till midnight and roasting apples. One night, I remember, it came out that, of about fifteen people round the fire, everyone except myself had been in prison. There were uproarious scenes in the village on Saturdays, for the people who had money used to get well drunk, and it needed the police to get them out of the pub. I have no doubt the residents thought us a nasty vulgar lot, but I could not help feeling that it was rather good for a dull village to have this invasion of cockneys once a year.

(from 'Hop-Picking', 1931)

Dry August and warm
Does harvest no harm.

A rainy Au-gust
Makes a hard bread crust.

Harvest Customs

CHRISTINA HOLE

Many of the old harvest customs have disappeared, though most farmers still provide a Mell or Harvest Supper for all their workers after the corn has been brought in. Mechanical reapers and binders have replaced the old hand sickles and have made unnecessary the Lord and Lady of the Harvest, who led the reapers and set the pace for the work. They have also done away with the concerted effort on the part of all concerned to get the last field cut before the neighbouring farmer could cut his, and the nominees shouted by the triumphant labourers when they had succeeded in the attempt, to the effect that 'This is to gie notice that Mr— has gi'en the seck a turn and sent t'owd hare into Mr—'s standing corn.' So, too, with the cutting of the last sheaf, once so important a part of the harvest rites; the machine takes it in its stride without the superstitious fear that formerly attended this part of the work. There was in every district a definite reluctance to be the one who cut the last handful, and to evade the undesirable distinction, the men took it in turns to throw their sickles at it. Sometimes a ribbon was tied loosely round the last remaining stalks, and the man who cut it was rewarded with a small sum of money. When the sheaf was eventually cut, it was tied up and decorated, or dressed in woman's clothes, and was brought in triumph to the farmhouse and set in a place of honour at the Mell supper. It was known as the Maiden, or the Kern Baby, or the Mare; the name given to it was always feminine because it represented the Corn Spirit, whose last refuge it had been while it was still standing in the field. In Scotland it was called the Maiden if it was cut before Hallowe'en and the Cailleach, or Old Woman, if it was cut after that date. But whatever its name it was sacred; it was dangerous to cut it but, once gathered, it was kept in the farmhouse throughout the year as a guarantee of continued fruitfulness in the fields and the success of next year's harvest.

(from *English Custom and Usage*, 1941)

The Harvest

ALISON UTTLEY

One day Roger barked with more than his accustomed fury, galloping in a semi-circle by the rose trees and barn, as he strained towards the hill and some distant sound. 'There's summat up,' observed Joshua to Dan, 'I shouldn't be surprised if it's the Irish.' He walked over to the bank and looked down the hill. A little procession of men swayed slowly up among the fragrant gorse and bushes of wild roses which lined the path. In their hands they carried bundles, in red and blue handkerchiefs, more baggage was slung on their backs, on rough sticks, and great loaves of bread were tucked under their arms. They smoked and spat, and waved their hats to Joshua as he leaned over the wall to greet them.

Tom came hurrying out when Dan ran breathless with the news, 'The Irish are here, they've come, Master.' The big gate opened and the file of men came straggling past the garden into the yard, down the path to the kitchen door, to pay their respects. Old Mike came first with his blue bundle in his thin brown hand. He was a small wiry man, with a face bright and keen as a bird's. He had piercing blue eyes under bushy eyebrows, uneven blackened teeth, and a pointed chin covered with stubble. He was a hard drinker and a hard worker, the men's acknowledged leader and arbitrator, a great talker and a fighter and a dancer. It was he who settled the men's wages with Tom Garland, and arranged the hours of work and the terms for wet days.

His place was on the haystack, to receive the hay from the great piled wains, pitched to him with the longest forks, for he could make a cleaner, tidier, and firmer stack than anyone in the countryside. When Old Mike had finished, his stacks looked like houses, with straight sides and neat gables, a particularly difficult task where the ground sloped and dipped as it did in the stack-yard.

His father had worked at Windystone, and his grandson

112

would come in a few years to take his place. He intended to mention him to Tom in good time.

Over a blue and white shirt, open at the neck, showing his hairy chest, he wore an old coat, green with age, a cast-off from the farm years ago. It was made of good strong broadcloth, and would last for many a season yet, but he expected with luck to get another for best from the farmer this year. His trousers were strapped at waist and ankle, and on his head he wore a black clerical hat, whose history was unknown, but he had worn it before Margaret was married, in rain, wind and sun, for many a year. It was inseparable from him, the badge which he removed perhaps when he slept, but certainly not during the day.

As he sat on the dresser with his back to the lustre jugs and priceless old china, sipping a basin of tea, and blowing the curling steam, a strong heady smell came from him in waves, travelling up to the ceiling and into every cranny and nook of the room, a smell of tobacco twist, corduroy, beer, and Ireland. Susan called it 'The Irishmen's Smell', and sniffed it up eagerly with mingled fear and delight.

After Old Mike came Young Mike, his son, a man in middle life, as silent as his father was talkative, an indeterminate man with a faint smile, not a particular friend of anyone's for he didn't work as hard as his father.

Malachi and Dominick, the twins, were slim young haymakers, good-looking, curly-haired, brown-skinned, with white even teeth and broad happy smiles. They were everybody's favourites and were a constant source of fun, they were so much alike. They kissed Susan, the only men whom she allowed that privilege, and gave her a penny with the Irishmen's smell all over it, which she kept in a little box, safe with its penetrating odour, to remind her of them when they were far away.

They asked after the Master's rheumatism, and told Margaret that she got younger every year. They smiled at Becky and joked her, as she hurried backwards and forwards between kitchen, pantry, and dairy, and out to the troughs. They patted Roger who quickly stopped barking and fawned upon them.

Next came Sheumas, old, quiet, dreamy, with a gentle

113

smile and far-away look. He was polite and timid, he drank very little and guarded his money most carefully to take back to Ireland. He looked frail, yet he worked longer than anyone. Tom thought he was a bit soft in the head, he was always the last, 'like a cow's tail', yet he was a good worker, clean and thorough.

The most important of the men were Patrick and Corney and Andy, the mowers. They were big, broad-shouldered, red-bearded men, relations of one another, brothers and cousins, quiet and courteous, but suddenly turning fierce and quarrelsome without any warning as they talked in Gaelic to one another. They were Susan's idea of brigands, or Assyrians sweeping down on the Israelites. They tied their corduroy trousers with twisted grass below the knee, to keep them out of the deep wet meadows, and at the backs of their leather belts they carried sockets holding their whet-stones. They brought their own scythes wrapped in sacking on their backs.

They all crowded into the already full kitchen and ducked their heads ceremoniously as they wished, 'Good luck to ye', and 'God bless ye', and 'Here's good health'. They brought meat in the great iron pot from their Place to be cooked on the stove, and their surplus bread to be kept in the pantry, out of the way of mice or rats. Through the wide-open door streamed the sunlight, dappling their trousers with golden discs.

The first night was spent over a few tots of beer from the barrel in the small barn. They sat outside in the evening sunshine, on long low forms near the door of their Place, telling tales of Ireland, of their wives, of the wage question, of cruel landlords and cattle-driving, and potato famine, which interested Tom extremely, and astonished Susan as she looked at their great frames and thought of the wild, savage, pagan land from which they had come, over the sea, like the summer birds.

Swallows and swifts hawked overhead, swooping down in frenzied rushes, chasing each other with shrill cries, dipping almost to the old hats rammed on the Irishmen's heads. They swept round the ancient buildings, over the grey-blue roofs, and the mossy gables with their stone balls, keeping ever near their human friends, excited and gay because the Irishmen had come and there would be companionship in the barns and cart-sheds.

The martins leaned out of their houses in the roof of the cart-shed, with their white breasts on their window-sills, joining in the cries of the birds and the talk of the men.

On a high bough in the orchard sang a thrush, the same fellow who came there every night. Tom used to sit listening as he watched for the Irishmen coming and waited for the weather to become settled and the grass to ripen, and the bird sang to him alone, its long wonderful song, which he repeated under his breath in the soft whistle the animals and birds loved.

Now the men were here, and he stopped them to listen. 'Hark to the throstle yonder,' he said, and they took their pipes from their mouths and sat silent whilst the bird sang, and the great moon came slowly from behind the wood, so near, only just across a little field.

Dusk fell, and bit-bats came from the old cart-sheds below the gate, perched on the side of the hill in a sheltered ledge. They hung all day in the roof, above the plough, the chain-harrow, the scarlet bonny rake, the rollers, and the deep blue and red hay-wains, but at night they came to hunt with the late swallows.

Susan waved her pinafore, to make them come to her hands, for she always wanted to catch one of these strange, wild, night creatures. They shot past her face, squeaking their tiny high cry, and their leather wings beat softly in the air, almost noiseless, but clear to her intense senses. She could see their unblinking eyes as she stretched out her hands, but they never stopped for her to catch one.

A nightjar whirred on the ground under the sycamore trees, and the moon rose high in the sky, shining through the dark firs.

'Good night, Dominick, good night, Malachi. Sweet repose, think of me, when you're under the clothes,' she called out as she went reluctantly to bed.

No candles were needed and as Susan undressed in the moonlight she smiled happily to think of the hay-makers and all the delight they were about to bring to the farm.

Becky, too, later on, in her little attic in the gable, looked at the moon through the skylight and sighed over Dominick's bright smile and Malachi's gay smile, and the easy country ways of her oatcake man, who certainly couldn't say the flattering things the Irishmen said.

Mrs Garland prayed long on her knees by the bed, with her hands folded on the patchwork quilt. She prayed for fine weather, for a speedy harvest, and God's blessing on the hay.

Tom Garland lay thinking of his fields, the Daisy Spot, with its rich heavy crop, the Ten-acre, of which the half on the high hillside was so short that it would barely pay for cutting. He thought of Whitewell field, with its hollows and hills, covered with sweet good grass, and Woodside, where the pheasants had made such havoc, trampling the grass with their long feet, of Top Pasture and Bottom Pasture, always fallow, of Harrowpiece, of Greeny Croft, and Silver Field, and Longside, and Four-ellums.

He turned uneasily as he thought of his own father, and his grandfather, lying in the same bedroom, planning, struggling through the years, from birth to death, ploughing, harrowing, harvesting.

There was little profit, but a blessed peace in this world high up, away from mithering blustering folk.

Old Joshua lay in his little room, listening to the owls which hooted over the barn roofs. The scent of honeysuckle poured in at his open window, bringing a sweet pain to his heart. He thought of his own farm, of his hopes at hay-time, under a moon like this. Old Mike had worked for him too, and he and his wife had prepared the little barn for his use, when he came with Andrew, long since dead. His orchard was full of bees, his garden full of roses, far more roses than ever there were at Windystone, and a grand red honeysuckle poked its long streamers through his small squares of windows, with regular crowns of flowers. But bad luck had always followed him, first his wife died, then his daughter had left him, accidents happened to his cattle, in field and wood, and he had bought a mare which turned lame the next day – all sorts of disasters came, till at last, daunted by Fate, he had sold up and given in. Well, he was glad, life wouldn't be long now. Perhaps this would be his last harvest, and then he would go to the Lord's harvest.

In the fields life went on, under the moon's white light. Field mice ran along their tiny green tunnels under the bending grass, to their nests, hollowed out among the roots, just below the level of the cruel scythe. Rabbits, unconscious of the morrow, played in the mowing grass, sitting up to bite sweet juicy blades, listening for the fox who stole along by the edge of the wood. Little winds blew the sorrel and swept over the tightly closed silky seeds of dandelion and hawkweed. Then the moon hid behind a rainbow cloud and the world fell asleep.

Morning came, cool, and sweet with bird-song and white mists. At five o'clock when the corncrake whirred in the Whitewell field and the cuckoo called on every side, the mowers were up and in the meadow. A soft rain fell, a good gentle rain, blessing the fields, and the dew lay thick over the grass. The three men stood on the path and sharpened their scythes, and Tom stood watching them. The music of the hone floated up the field, in at the bedroom windows, ringing a strange familiar note which came into Susan's dreams and made her smile in her sleep.

They took their positions, Patrick first, then Corney, and last Andy, and they stayed in this order during the whole of the mowing, each mowing his own lane through the grass, yet overlapping by the tip of the scythe, so that not a blade of grass remained. The long rhythmic swish, swish, swish, filled the air, as the three men, with bodies curved and motion even and regular, worked, their strong arms sweeping the shining blade through the silken grass. Their voices, murmuring in Gaelic, made a bass accompaniment to the treble of the scythes. Their feet swung outward in time to the cut of the scythe, and behind them they left three deep swathes, pale green, and soft-coloured as the rain. Now and again they stood upright and wiped the blade with a wisp of grass before they honed it afresh with the stone which they carried on their backs.

At seven they came back for breakfast, of bread and fat bacon which Becky had boiled the night before, washed down with a jug of strong tea, with sugar and milk. The hay-makers had breakfast with them and then went away for two days, to work on a small farm over the hill, until enough grass had been cut at Windystone.

After breakfast, when Dan had gone with the milk, Tom and Joshua brought out the mowing machine, clattering and clacking from the cart-shed. Last year the farmer had bought it, for use in the few level parts of the fields, and on the gentler slopes. Often the wet had caught them before the Irishmen had finished and with the machine he could speed up the mowing. The mowers took the high steep field, where the machine could not climb. They swept under the hedges round the smooth meadows, where the ground always rose steeply, they mowed over the ditches and by the streams and springs, in soft ground and by the troughs, on the slopes of the stiff hills, round groves of trees, and the boles of the great isolated beeches and ashes and elms, which stood in the fields. Most of the work was done by the mowers, the machine could not cut clean on those curving, steep hills.

All day they worked, returning only for meals to their Place. The fallen grass lay in even swathes, in broad, coloured parallel stripes on a pale green robe, white dog-daisies, red sorrel, purple vetch mixed with the deep blue of wild geranium, and the yellows of buttercup and dandelion, lying on the short pale grass.

Over the horse's eyes hung a leafy branch of ash, to keep away the flies, but the men worked on, each with his accompanying halo of dancing insects.

Now a rabbit darted out and the mowers dropped their scythes with wild yells, and threw their hats at the bewildered animal which doubled backwards and forwards among them until with bare hands they caught and throttled it. Often a rabbit's legs were cut off with the scythe, and then it only staggered a few yards before they killed it. They were put beside the men's coats and carried back for a stew. Hedgehogs, too, were caught by the busy mowers, and roasted on little stick fires, when they tasted like chicken.

Field-mice, long-legged frogs, solemn toads, were disturbed, and fled past Susan who hurried down to the fields when she came home from school and ate her tea in the grass. But sometimes a wasps' nest or even a hornets' nest hole turned the tables and made the Irishmen run.

Round and round went the mowing machine, encircling a piece of meadow land, and the little creatures who lived in it retreated further into the middle. The loud whirr and buzz of the machine terrified them, they knew not from which direction it came, and they lay trembling in the deep grass. As the island became smaller the mowers came up with cudgels from the wood-stack. They stood round ready for the frantic flight of rabbits which came as the grass disappeared. There was pandemonium for a few moments, they yelled and bellowed, to confuse the lost, startled animals, and then a heap of furry bodies smeared with blood lay on the ground.

When the hay-makers returned, with merry talk and much laughter, with the clinking of tin mugs, and the rattle of chains and harness, they went into the fields to ted the grass.

Days of hard work followed, long days, from dewy cool mornings before the sun rose behind the steep hills, to dusk when the bit-bats came out and flew over the haymakers' heads. The house doors were all locked and Susan stayed away from school to her great delight to go with Becky and Margaret, each in a pink, lilac, or buff-coloured sun-bonnet,

119

and a pale holland frock, to work in the fields. Margaret did not stay long, but Becky and Susan worked all day, running errands and haymaking. The mowers were well ahead, but the haymakers came after, tedding the grass with their forks, and spreading it to dry, then raking it into long lines, one behind another, each making his own swathes which curved over the hills, down the hollows, and up the little slopes till they faded away among the thin grass at the top.

Susan was for the first time in her life allowed to use a rake, one a little smaller than the others, which she slowly pulled over the hay, careful lest a tooth should be broken out, or a piece of hay should be left lying loose on the green grass.

In the next field the tedders were tossing, and in the field beyond the mowers were honing their scythes and then bending over their heavy grass. The sun beat down and dried the hay, bringing out the hidden scents, the clean delicious odours which so soon follow the pungent strong smell of cut grass.

So they travelled from field to field, uncovering all the hidden secrets of the individual meadows, the patch of rosy ragged robin, in the little marsh, the white pool of dog-daisies, the hedge covered with honeysuckle, the round nest of field-mice with pink, curled, little bodies, the water-troughs which had been so long unused that they were now hidden under the surrounding ferns. Susan left the haymakers to run after the mowers, who were the first to find all the treasures, but, heedless, they moved steadily forward, and she hunted alone until her father called her back to bring them a drink.

By the open gates, where the little blue butterflies lived all the summer, on the shady side of the hedge, the drinks lay. Great old wicker-covered bottles, and a brown oval jar, covered with crosses and flowers like an embroidered quilt, were filled with beer and carried proudly by the Irishmen in the morning. By the side lay the tot, a pewter drinking cup. Old Mike called the halt for a drink and Tom gave his consent, looking up at the sun, and calculating the time since the last tot. The beer was never left in the field with the men alone, after one disastrous day a few years before. Tom poured out the beer and the tot passed round, whilst the men wiped their foreheads and shook sweat off their necks.

Tom and Joshua drank tea from a large white jug, with a cup over the top, or sometimes they had oatmeal water, or dandelion beer which Becky had made a short time before, very sweet and pleasant. Susan ran with the jug to her father and Becky, or went all the way back over the fields to the house for more. Inside it was cool and strange, the blinds were drawn in the parlours and the sunlight danced through their whiteness, flickering on the furniture. The rooms were talking again, and she stopped to tell the news of the fields to the ghosts of the house, to the listening shadows, which waited expectantly when she entered. Margaret filled up the jugs, and gave her a little sugar-cone bag full of oatmeal and brown sugar from the two big glazed mugs on the pantry shelf. She took a toy spoon from her doll cupboard and ate the feast before she went out again to the fields, walking carefully and slowly lest she should spill the tea which 'swaled' in the jug.

At milking-time Dan and Joshua left off, but Tom worked with the men, only stopping for a bite of food, and then on again. The long lines were pushed downhill and made into cocks, first little ones and then two or three were joined together to form great cocks, like small stacks. If rain threatened everybody rushed to cock the hay, and sometimes days were spent in cocking to keep out the wet, and tedding the hay out again to get it thoroughly dry.

Tom and Old Mike laid the straddles and prepared for the stacks. Then one fine day loading began, and the two haywains were brought out. Tom Garland and Dan led the two mares, Duchess and Diamond, with the loads of hay up the hills to the stack-yard where Old Mike waited. When a cart was piled with a mountain of hay, ropes were thrown over to keep the load from slipping off as the mares struggled to the stack-yard.

'Pull! Pull! Pull! Pull agen! Pull agen! Agen! and Agen! And agen!' sounded through the summer air like a sea-shanty as the Irishmen strained at the ropes to tighten the mass. Then the man on the top slid down and the perilous ascent began.

The two mares strained at the great load, and men pushed behind as the cart moved up the hills. Tom led one mare and Dan the other, encouraging, helping, and resting, when there was a chance in the slope of the field. Other men hung like flies on one side to keep the top-heavy load from tumbling over and falling down the field. It was always an anxious time, a slip and a man and mare might be killed. Only the steady-going mares could be used, the pony was too frisky, although she was often put between the two, when the hill was especially difficult, and the horse was needed for other work.

Sweat poured down the men's faces and splashed on the ground, their shirts were soaked, their arms were taut and knotted with thick veins. Old Mike stood high on the sweet-scented stack, watching the hay-cart appear and disappear, like a ship in a rough sea, as it climbed up hills and sank into hollows. Always the voices came through the crystal air, singing across meadow and wood.

'Dimond! Dimond! Pull! Pull! Dimond! Duchess!' The mares, with heads stretched forward and the muscles of their great flanks quivering, corded, stretched, pulled with all their might, and the men exhorted them, putting every ounce of strength to task.

Shouting, sweating, the load reaches the top. Men pause to draw their hands across their faces and wring off the water, whilst they look at the bitter track up which they have fought their way. The mares tremble and Tom soothes them and strokes their wet sides. Then they start again, the last fifty yards up a gentler slope to the stack-yard, and everyone asks for a tot as the animals rest and eat a bundle of hay.

So it went on, and the fields were emptied of their burdens. One of the men walked up and down with the bonny-rake, collecting all the scraps left from loading and men went around the hedges cleaning everywhere up. Susan rode back each time in the empty cart, clinging to the side of the jolting wain, which jerked over lumps and into hollows and threatened to throw her out. But she sang a paean of joy, for this was the most beautiful thing in the world, better than a circus or a fair.

On Saturday nights the double doors of the big cart-shed were opened wide and the Irishmen gave a concert of song and dance.

Dominick was the chief singer, and he stood in front of the doors on the cobbles, whilst the song rolled on, verse after verse, none of which Susan understood. Then Old Mike danced, with great clatter of heels and swinging of arms. The others sat motionless, with their eyes fixed on his feet, which twinkled in an astonishing way for one so old. They interrupted with cries of 'Bravo, bravo!' and Old Mike's blue eyes stared across the fields to the beech wood as if he saw his own Galway mountains up there.

One after another they danced and sang, and joined in the merry choruses with stamping feet and shaking shoulders.

Sometimes Tom Garland brought out his concertina and played the airs they sang, or he gave them a hymn tune and they listened attentively. The darkness came down like a blue cloud, bit-bats flew in and out of the pitch-black shed, and screech-owls hooted in the fir trees. In the nearest fields, pale green and emptied of hay, the mares could be heard softly whinnying with pleasure, as they took their week-end rest. They knew as well as anyone that whatever the weather, however urgent the need for speed in the harvesting, nothing would be done on Sunday and they were free.

Becky sat with Susan on the wall joining in a hymn, clapping and listening to the concert which was the only kind she knew.

On Sundays the men fetched buckets of hot water from the kitchen boiler and borrowed razors and soap. They retired to a little field, mockingly called, 'The Forty-Acre Field', and there they washed their bodies, and shaved off the week's growth of beard. They put on clean shirts and trousers from their bundles, in the manger of the cow-house, and tied clean bright handkerchiefs round their necks. Then they washed their dirty shirts and hung them on the hedges and bushes to dry.

When they were clean and trim and all prinked out, they went off to Mass at a church six miles away, where the priest loved these children from over the sea, and welcomed them as they waited at the door for the fine folk to enter first.

But in the farm kitchen the great iron pot simmered and bubbled over the bright fire with the Irishmen's dinner inside, which Dominick and Patrick would soon carry to the little home in the cattle-stall.

(from *The Country Child*, 1931)

*

September blow soft
Until apples are in loft.

If it thunders on All Fool's Day
It brings good crops of corn and hay.

Cut your thistles before St John,
You must have two instead of one.

A good October and a good blast
To blow the hogs acorns and mast.

November

He has hanged himself – the Sun.
    He dangles
A scarecrow in thin air.

He is dead for love – the Sun,
    He who in forest tangles
Wooed all things fair.

That great lover – the Sun,
    Now spangles
The wood with blood-stains.

He has hanged himself – the Sun.
    How thin he dangles
In these grey rains!

F. W. HARVEY

Here's to thee, old apple tree,
Whence thou may'st bud
And whence thou may'st blow,
And whence thou may'st bear apples enow:
Hats full and caps full,
Bushels full and sacks full,
And my pockets full, too.

Blow, Blow, Thou Winter Wind

Blow, blow, thou winter wind,
Thou art not so unkind
   As man's ingratitude;
Thy tooth is not so keen,
Because thou art not seen,
   Although thy breath be rude.
Heigh-ho! sing, heigh-ho! unto the green holly:
Most friendship is feigning, most loving mere folly:
   Then, heigh-ho, the holly!
    This life is most jolly.

Freeze, freeze, thou bitter sky,
That dost not bite so nigh
   As benefits forgot:
Though thou the waters warp,
Thy sting is not so sharp
   As friend remember'd not.
Heigh-ho! sing, heigh-ho! unto the green holly:
Most friendship is feigning, most loving mere folly:
   Then, heigh-ho, the holly!
    This life is most jolly.

(from *As You Like It*) WILLIAM SHAKESPEARE

Snow

No breath of wind,
No gleam of sun –
Still the white snow
Swirls softly down –
Twig and bough
And blade and thorn
All in an icy
Quiet, forlorn.
Whispering, nestling,
Through the air,
On sill and stone,
Roof – everywhere,

It heaps its powdery
Crystal flakes,
Of every tree
A mountain makes;
Till pale and faint
At shut of day,
Stoops from the West
One wintry ray,
And, feathered in fire,
Where ghosts the moon,
A robin shrills
His lonely tune.

WALTER DE LA MARE

A Country Calendar

With traditional illustrations

Holidays with pay are by no means the purely modern arrangement we are inclined to suppose. Over many past centuries the year was broken up by numberless festivals that gave workers all sorts of days off. If these were all strung together they would add up to an impressive period of relaxation, even though not every kind of worker was covered by every kind of feast.

Holiday means holy day, so fairly obviously at one time most of the year's festivals had a religious turn. Not only important times like Christmas and Easter offered their festivities, but dozens of saints' days. Few are honoured now – though we do, perhaps, spare a thought for St George, St David, St Andrew and St Patrick; and St Swithin hangs on, too, being a weatherman. Some of the feasts of early times were left over from more ancient days still, but had been made respectable by some new name. The pagan rites of Midsummer, for instance, were Christianized by being tied to the feast of St John.

Over the years, many changes have come to public holidays. At the time of the Reformation the saints fell into disrepute and many of their festivals were discontinued; and during the Commonwealth the Puritans did away with a lot of holiday fun, frowning on dancing, banishing the maypole and play acting – of which there was always a lot at fairs. Some of these frivolities were revived at a later date.

We still have survivors of some ancient fairs to be seen in different parts of the British Isles. There's the Goose Fair at Nottingham, which originally honoured the feast of St Michael; and we do still talk of a Michaelmas goose. There's still the Cuckoo Fair at Heathfield in Sussex, and this is probably older than the saints, for it celebrates the arrival of the cuckoo, which is said to be let out of a basket on the 14th April by a mysterious old woman who has charge of all the cuckoos.

128

A complete survey of all the holiday business over hundreds of years, and in every corner of the country, fills whole volumes. This *Country Calendar* is to give just an impression of how full the year used to be.

*

1 January. New Year's Day

New Year's Day was full of excitements – much singing, much dancing, much eating, much drinking, and different traditions from one county to the next. In some parts the Lord of the Manor received dues on this day for certain rights of common and grazing. There were mummers' plays, blackened faces, many tricks played on the unwary. In the west country and other parts, too, it was considered wise to make a gift of honey to the bees; in other parts mistletoe hung in the house for Christmas was taken down and given to the first cow to calve in the New Year – that insured good fortune to the whole dairy for the coming twelvemonth. On New Year's Day nothing should be thrown out of doors, not even the ashes, but something green and living must be taken in. Letting in the New Year, first-footing by a dark man or boy, the carrying of coal and bread over the threshold remain to this day, though such customs are no longer a part of rural life in which all the village joins as a matter of course.

6 January. Twelfth Night

On this night the revels were many and varied – the drinking of wassail, a very ancient brew indeed, the cutting of a huge rich cake with a bean in it, the finder of the bean being made King of the Revels; also of course much dancing and singing. The owners of orchards drank health to their apple trees, to ensure a good crop. Fires were lit, twelve small, standing for the Twelve Days of Christmas, and one big one in honour of Twelfth Night itself. Some charities gave out their 'dole' on Twelfth Night. The calendar was adjusted by law in 1752, but some people stuck obstinately to the old dating, and for them 6th January was known as Old Christmas Eve.

2 February. Candlemas

The feast of the Purification of the Virgin Mary, a very important church festival. Candles and wax tapers to be used during the year were blessed by the priest. The congregation carried lighted candles in procession round the church. Such candles, taken home, were believed by country folk to ward off evil spirits. Many fairs were held on this day.

14 February. St Valentine

Patron saint of lovers – because on this date of the year every bird is said to choose its mate. A girl's future husband could be the man she met first on St Valentine's Day. At one time it became the custom to give presents on the day – often extremely costly ones. There were many Valentine Fairs – notably one at King's Lynn in Norfolk which went on for six days. Of course business was done at  fairs then as now, when we have our big agricultural shows.

1 March. St David

The patron saint of Wales was honoured in all other parts of the British Isles. Old verses give advice to farmers – on St David's they must sow beans and peas, as well as oats and barley. Geese should be laying – if they are good geese. The 1st March was also considered the day on which *fleas swarmed*!

25 March. Lady Day

What we think of as *quarter-day*, when rents and bills must be paid, was a serious and important church feast – the feast of the Annunciation, or the day the angel Gabriel spoke to the Virgin Mary of what was in store for her. Hiring Fairs were held on Lady Day. Girls hoping to be hired as servants took up their stand in groups in the nearest market place.

1 April.   All Fools

No one seems quite sure where All Fools Day originated –
some say it came from ancient Rome. Certainly it is celebrated, and always has been, in other countries than our own.
April Fool customs were much the same in the past as they
are in the present – except that then there were more of
them and the whole day seemed much more important.

23 April.   St George

Patron saint of England – no one pretending for a moment
that he killed his dragon anywhere but in the Middle East.
There were solemn ceremonies as well as secular gaieties on
this day right down into modern times. Fairs were numerous,
some of them lasting as long as nine days. Even today, we
sometimes remember to fly the flag of St George on churches
and public buildings. Well within memory it was the custom
to honour the day by wearing a red rose.

25 April.   St Mark's Eve

Another of those eves on which young girls sought by
fantastic means to divine the time of their marriage and the
name of the groom. More gruesomely, if you watched the
graveyard on St Mark's Eve you would see the 'ghosts' of
those to die during the following year.

1 May.   May Day

Parties of men and women, boys and girls went out in the
early morning 'a-maying', bringing home green boughs and
wild flowers to deck their homes. May Day festivities ranged
from revels of an elaborate nature at Court, to simple rustic
frivolities. 'When not employed in collecting the produce of
the fields and woods, the Mayers spent their time in horn-
blowing, singing, dancing, playing on whistles, flutes and
violins, or enjoying light refreshments.' (A. R. Wright,
British Calendar Customs, pub. The Folklore Society).
Although the Puritans put an end to the fun, it all came back
again after the Restoration of the Monarchy. Today May

Day has become a political holiday – but that happened for the first time in 1517, when anti-alien riots were arranged to coincide with May Day; a good many rioters were executed. Besides all the jollities of the best kind of country May Day, people lit fires as a form of protection against evil, or made crosses of hawthorn and hung them above the house and stable doors to fend off witches.

11 June.   St Barnabas

There used to be great festivities in England on St Barnabas day – decorating of churches with roses and lavender, the making of bowers of oak, which in some parts stayed all the year round. All about the country were great fairs, usually called Barnaby Fair. The ladybird is nicknamed Bishop Barnaby in some parts of Sussex, but why it should be so no one seems able to explain.

23 and 24 June.   Midsummer Eve and Midsummer Day

Or St John's Eve and the Feast of St John. It is a very, very ancient feast, kept by the Druids at the very least. On the Eve many great fires were lighted. Sometimes people believed that leaping through the flames would ward off evil spirits. Bonfire may mean *bonefire*, for that was the fuel used at one time. This was another of those times when girls liked to discover whom they might marry. If a girl hung her chemise inside-out over a chair in front of a fire, her future husband would come in and turn it right side out again! Or if they wore a rose and went to church at midnight, then their 'intended' would snatch it away. There are so many customs that attach to Midsummer that it is pretty well impossible to list them. It was a time of both mystery and merriment.

29 June. 6 July. SS Peter and Paul

The 29th June is the true feast, the 6th July is the *octave* of the feast, according to church dating. But both days are days for the ceremony of Rush-bearing. On this day, when rushes were used on floors, they were renewed and a great cleansing took place. Also there were bonfires again, and lambs roasted whole, and offerings of venison made to lords, bishops and abbots. In Devon they made a huge plum pudding and dragged it in triumph to the feasting place. In coastal places, of course, there was blessing of the nets, St Peter being patron of fishermen.

15 July. St Swithin

It was said that when the bones of this saint were moved from the churchyard and freshly and grandly entombed in the newly built cathedral at Winchester, 'the saint wept'. After that it was, apparently, dry for forty days. Some believe that the legend of forty days wet, if it is wet on St Swithin's Day, arose out of this event. But it really makes rather little sense. An important ceremony, however, was the christening of the apples on this day, and no apple was plucked or eaten before this date (it would have been pretty hard and sour so early, surely). The custom, however, is remembered in many parts of the country.

28 July. St James

The new style calendar puts St James's feast on the 5th August, and fairs were held on either day, according to the leaning of the locality. Oysters were first eaten on St James's (or *Sanjam* in some areas). Children collected the oyster shells and made *grottos*. These were set up by the roadside and the children collected pennies from passers, in much the same way as they still do in the days leading up to the 5th November, in honour of the *guy*. In old pictures of the saint himself, in church windows, say, he is shown with a scallop or oyster shell.

29 September.   St Michael

Michaelmas is still an important time, covering a law term. It is a *quarter-day*, a time for the paying of bills. It could also be called the end of summer, the start of winter, a time for gathering in. Many ancient customs attach to Michaelmas, but the one everybody recalls is the tradition of eating roast goose. Geese are in their prime at this season, so no doubt the custom arose from this simple fact. A goose, too, was often among tithes paid by tenants to their landlords at this time. Many hiring fairs took place at Michaelmas, when men and girls settled their employment for the coming twelve-month. Every man or maid carried the emblem of his trade, and such fairs were called Mop Fairs, or just plain Mops.

18 October.   St Luke

St Luke is the patron saint of doctors, but the customs celebrating his feast seem designed to injure rather than to heal. Parsons were pelted with apples – dogs were whipped through the streets in Yorkshire. Girls employed sinister charms for the usual purpose of finding a husband. Fairs were rather specialized – the Horn Fair, selling articles made of horn and including revels of a somewhat free and easy order. Then there was the Dish Fair, selling articles made all of wood. There is often a spell of fine warm weather at this time, known as St Luke's Little Summer.

25 October.   St Crispin

This day was very much a Shoemakers' Holiday, St Crispin being their patron. It is sometimes called Snobs' Holiday, since *snob* is an old word for shoemaker. Processions featured in many places. In one such St Crispin rode in armour followed by his troops, with drums banging and trumpets blowing. Perhaps this might be in memory of the fact that the battle of Agincourt was fought on St Crispin's Day, as Shakespeare will not let us forget. A rhyme for the day goes thus:

> On the 25th of October
> Curs't be the cobbler
> Who goes to bed sober!

31 October. All Hallow E'en

The eve of All Souls, a ghostly occasion, pretty sinister in those times when witches were something more than fairy-tale figures. We keep up some of the customs still, though in a somewhat half-hearted fashion. Bobbing for apples is still a feature of Hallow E'en parties. Innumerable ways of knowing your sweetheart were practised on this night – the simplest is that familiar one of peeling an apple round and round, flinging the core over your shoulder, then turning quickly to see what initial it has formed on hitting the ground. At one time a girl put a crooked sixpence and a sprig of rosemary under her pillow to dream of her future husband. The fire must not be let out on Hallow E'en, for fire is a very powerful charm against witches. In fact, almost every superstition ever heard of is somehow linked with this feast.

1 November. All Saints

or *All Hallows* (that is Hallowed or Holy persons)
There are really three days concerned in this festival – Hallow E'en, or the *eve* of All Saints; All Saints itself, which is also the eve of All Souls; and All Souls Day, when the dead are remembered and mourned. All Saints was one of the more important church festivals. On this day country children and town children alike carried out the strange custom called *Souling.* They went singing from house to house, wishing good fortune to the inmates, and begging in return a 'soul-cake'; with time, whatever they were given was called by this name.

11 November. St Martin

Like St Luke, St Martin gives his name to a spell of unseasonable summery weather. Martinmas was another rent-paying day. It was a time for buying in winter provisions, and besides the usual good dinner after a visit to church, there were in different parts of the country many curious customs that are hard to define. A certain fine paid to a noble landlord on this day could have a substitute, if the debtor was able to find such a beast as a white bull with a red nose and red ears – or in another part of the country, with red tipped ears and a red tipped tail. Martinmas was also another day for hiring servants – called Pack-rag Day, from the fact that servants packed up their belongings and moved to fresh employment.

23 November. St Clement   25 November. St Catherine

The patron saint of blacksmiths. Children went *Clemening* in much the same way that they went *souling*, and on St Catherine's day *Catherning* . . . Sometimes the song of the day puts the two saints together as in:

> Catteny, Clemeny, year by year,
> Some of your apples and some of your beer . . .

St Catherine is the patron saint of lacemakers and spinners – or *spinsters*, which comes about because she was herself an unmarried lady, a martyr for her faith, being nastily killed by a method popular in her day, which involved being bound to a wheel. Hence *Catherine Wheel*.

30 November.   St Andrew

Some lacemakers preferred St Andrew to St Catherine for a patron; and he is of course patron saint of Scotland. Festivities are of a familiar kind, but include some less well known. An unpleasant custom was *Hunting the Squirrel*, but it was not only squirrels that were massacred by boys and men roaring through the woods with cudgels and staves intent on destruction. On this day schoolchildren indulged in the custom of *barring-out*. They rushed into the schoolhouse and locked it against the master. The scholars then demanded holidays, the schoolmaster agreed, and all ended most amiably.

These are by no means all the days that were called holy in the course of the year in past times. It must be remembered that work then was from dawn till dusk, whatever the time of year and length of day, so that the breaks were not only welcome but necessary. Besides the saints' days, which are overtaken after St Andrew by Advent and the approach of Christmas, there are the twelve days of Christmas itself, Shrovetide, Easter, Ascensiontide, Whitsuntide. All these have customs besides purely religious ones – such as *Beating the Bounds* at Rogationtide, between Ascension and Whitsun. And there was *Mothering Sunday* and Hocktide and Trinity Monday; and *Well-dressing* around Ascension, and all the dolegiving ceremonies attached to Maundy Thursday; not to mention pancakes on Shrove Tuesday . . . Perhaps it is all these feasts, so jovial and goodnatured, that bring to mind the picture of Merry England that was popular until people began to inquire more closely about the poverty and cruelty and injustice of those times. All the same, there must have been great pleasure to be had from the fairs and the feasting.

(compiled from *British Calendar Customs*, A. R. WRIGHT)

THE HUNT

What Shall He Have that Kill'd the Deer?

What shall he have that kill'd the deer?
His leather skin and horns to wear.
    Then sing him home:
Take thou no scorn to wear the horn;
It was a crest ere thou wast born:
    Thy father's father wore it,
    And thy father bore it:
The horn, the horn, the lusty horn
Is not a thing to laugh to scorn.

(from *As You Like It*)   WILLIAM SHAKESPEARE

A Medieval Hunt

Translated from Middle English by Brian Stone

In the faint light before dawn folk were stirring;
Guests who had to go gave orders to their grooms,
Who busied themselves briskly with the beasts, saddling,
Trimming their tackle and tying on their luggage.
Arrayed for riding in the richest style,
Guests leaped on their mounts lightly, laid hold of their
    bridles,
And each rider rode out on his own chosen way.
The beloved lord of the land was not the last up,
Being arrayed for riding with his retinue in force.
He ate a sop hastily when he had heard mass,
And hurried with horn to the hunting field;
Before the sun's first rays fell on the earth,
On their high steeds were he and his knights.
Then these cunning hunters came to couple their hounds,
Cast open the kennel doors and called them out,
And blew on their bugles three cold notes.
The hounds broke out barking, baying fiercely,
And when they went chasing, they were whipped back.
There were a hundred choice huntsmen there, whose fame
    Resounds.
  To their stations keepers strode;
  Huntsmen unleashed hounds:
  The forest overflowed
  With the strident bugle sounds.
At the first cry wild creatures quivered with dread.
The deer in distraction darted down the dales
Or up to the high ground, but eagerly they were
Driven back by the beaters, who bellowed lustily.
They let the harts with high-branching heads have their
    freedom,
And the brave bucks, too, with their broad antlers,
For the noble prince had expressly prohibited

141

Meddling with male deer in the months of close season.
But the hinds were held back with a 'Hey!' and a 'Whoa!'
And does driven with much din to the deep valleys.
Lo! the shimmering of the shafts as they were shot from
    bows!
An arrow flew forth at every forest turning,
The broad head biting on the brown flank.
They screamed as the blood streamed out, sank dead on
    the sward,
Always harried by hounds hard on their heels,
And the hurrying hunter's high horn notes.
Like the rending of ramped hills roared the din.
If one of the wild beasts slipped away from the archers
After being dragged from the high ground and harried to
    the water,
It was dragged down and met death at the dog-bases,
So skilled were the hunt-servants at stations lower down,
So gigantic the greyhounds that grabbed them in a flash,
Seizing them savagely, as swift, I swear,
        As sight.
    The lord, in humour high,
    Would spur, then stop and alight.
    In bliss the day went by
    Till dark grew on, and night . . .

(from *Sir Gawain and the Green Knight*)

The Children of the New Forest

CAPTAIN MARRYAT

As soon as dinner was over, Edward and Humphrey took down their guns, having agreed that they would go and hunt the wild cattle.

'Humphrey, have you any idea where the herd of cattle are feeding at this time?'

'I know where they were feeding yesterday and the day before, and I do not think that they will have changed their ground; for the grass is yet very young, and only grown on the southern aspects. Depend upon it, we shall fall in with them not four miles from where we now are, if not nearer.'

'We must stalk them as we do the deer, must we not? They won't allow us to approach within shot, Humphrey, will they?' said Edward.

'We have to take our chance, Edward; they will allow us to advance within shot, but the bulls will then advance upon us, while the herd increase their distance. On the other hand, if we stalk them, we may kill one, and then the report of the gun will frighten the others away. In the first instance there is a risk; in the second there is none, but there is more fatigue and trouble. Choose as you please; I will act as you decide.'

'Well, Humphrey, since you give me the choice, I think that this time I shall take the bull by the horns, as the saying is – that is, if there are any trees near us, for if the herd are in an open place I would not run such a risk; but if we can fire upon them and fall back upon a tree in case of a bull charging, I will take them openly.'

'With all my heart, Edward: I think it will be very hard, if, with our two guns and Smoker to back us, we do not manage to be masters of the field. However, we must survey well before we make our approach; and if we can get within shot without alarming or irritating them, we of course do so.'

'The bulls are very savage at this spring-time,' observed Edward.

'They are so at all times, as far as I can see of them,'

replied Humphrey; 'but we are near to them now I should think – yes, there is the herd.'

'There they are, sure enough,' replied Edward: 'now we have not to do with deer, and need not be so very cautious; but still the animals are wary, and keep a sharp lookout. We must approach them quietly, by slipping from tree to tree. Smoker, to heel! – down – quiet, Smoker – good dog!'

Edward and Humphrey stopped to load their guns, and then approached the herd in the manner which had been proposed, and were very soon within two hundred yards of the cattle, behind a large oak, when they stopped to reconnoitre. The herd contained about seventy head of cattle of various sizes and ages. They were feeding in all directions, scattered, as the young grass was very short; but although the herd was spread over many acres of land, Edward pointed out to Humphrey that all the full-grown large bulls were on the outside, as if ready to defend the others in case of attack.

'Humphrey,' said Edward, 'one thing is clear – as the herd is placed at present we must have a bull or nothing. It is impossible to get within shot of the others without passing a bull, and depend upon it our passage will be disputed; and moreover, the herd will take to flight, and we shall get nothing at all.'

'Well,' replied Humphrey, 'beef is beef; and, as they say, beggars must not be choosers, so let it be a bull, if it must be so.'

'Let us get nearer to them, and then we will decide what we shall do. Steady, Smoker!'

They advanced gradually, hiding from tree to tree, until they were within eighty yards of one of the bulls. The animal did not perceive them, and as they were now within range, they again stepped behind the tree to consult.

'Now, Edward, I think that it would be best to separate. You can fire from where we are, and I will crawl through the fern, and get behind another tree.'

'Very well, do so,' replied Edward; 'if you can manage, get to that tree with the low branches and then perhaps you will be within shot of the white bull, which is coming down in this direction. Smoker, lie down! He cannot go with you, Humphrey, it will not be safe.'

The distance of the tree which Humphrey ventured to get to was about one hundred and fifty yards from where Edward was standing. Humphrey crawled along for some time in the fern, but at last he came to a bare spot of about ten yards wide, which they were not aware of, and where he could not be concealed. Humphrey hesitated, and at last decided upon attempting to cross it. Edward, who was one moment watching the motions of Humphrey and at another those of the two animals nearest to them, perceived that the white bull farthest from him, but nearest Humphrey, threw its head in the air, pawed with its foot, and then advanced with a roar to where Humphrey was on the ground, still crawling towards the tree, having passed the open spot, and being now not many yards from the tree. Perceiving the danger that his brother was in, and that, moreover, Humphrey was not aware of it, he hardly knew how to act. The bull was too far from him to fire at it with any chance of success; and how to let Humphrey know that the animal had discovered him and was making towards him, without calling out, he did not know. All this was the thought of a moment, and then Edward determined to fire at the bull nearest to him, which he had promised not to do till Humphrey was also ready to fire; and after firing, to call Humphrey. He, therefore, for one moment turned away from his brother, and, taking aim at the bull, fired his gun; but probably from his nerves being a little shaken at the idea of Humphrey being in danger, the wound was not mortal, and the bull galloped back to the herd, which formed a close phalanx about a quarter of a mile distant. Edward turned to where his brother was, and perceived that the bull had not made off with the rest of the cattle, but was within thirty yards of Humphrey, and advancing upon him, and that Humphrey was standing up beside the tree with his gun ready to fire. Humphrey fired and, as it appeared, he also missed his aim; the animal made at him; but Humphrey, with great quickness, dropped his gun, and, swinging by the lower boughs, was into the tree, and out of the bull's reach in a moment. Edward smiled when he perceived that Humphrey was safe; but still he was a prisoner, for the bull went round and round the tree roaring and looking up at Humphrey. Edward thought a minute, then loaded his gun,

and ordered Smoker to run in to the bull. The dog, who had only been restrained by Edward's keeping him down at his feet, sprang forward to the attack. Edward had intended, by calling to the dog, to induce the bull to follow it till within gunshot; but before the bull had been attacked, Edward observed that one or two more bulls had left the herd, and were coming at a rapid pace towards him. Under these circumstances Edward perceived that his only chance was to climb into a tree himself, which he did, taking good care to take his gun and ammunition with him. Having safely fixed himself on a forked bough, Edward then surveyed the position of the parties. There was Humphrey in the tree, without his gun. The bull who had pursued Humphrey was now running at Smoker, who appeared to be aware that he was to decoy the bull towards Edward, for he kept retreating towards him. In the meantime the two other bulls were quite close at hand, mingling their bellowing and roaring with the first; and one of them as near to Edward as the first bull, which was engaged with Smoker. At last one of the advancing bulls stood still, pawing the ground as if disappointed at not finding an enemy, not forty yards from where Edward was perched. Edward took good aim, and when he fired the bull fell dead. Edward was reloading his piece when he heard a howl, and looking round saw Smoker flying up in the air, having been tossed by the first bull; and at the same time he observed that Humphrey had descended from the tree, recovered his gun, and was now safe again upon the lower bough. The first bull was advancing again to attack Smoker, who appeared incapable of getting away, so much was he injured by the fall, when the other bull, who apparently must have been an old antagonist of the first, roared and attacked him; and now the two boys were up in the tree, the two bulls fighting between them, and Smoker lying on the ground, panting and exhausted. As the bulls, with locked horns, were furiously pressing each other, both guns were discharged, both animals fell. After waiting a little while to see if they rose again, or if any more of the herd came up, Edward and Humphrey descended from the trees and heartily shook hands.

(from *The Children of the New Forest*, 1847)

147

Badger

When midnight comes a host of dogs and men
Go out and track the badger to his den;
And put a sack within the hole, and lie
Till the old grunting badger passes by.
He comes and hears – they let the strongest loose.
The old fox hears the noise and drops the goose.
The poacher shoots and hurries from the cry.
And the old hare, half wounded buzzes by.
They get a forked stick to bear him down
And clap the dogs and take him to the town,
And bait him all the day with many dogs,
And laugh and shout and fright the scampering hogs.
He runs along and bites at all he meets;
They shout and hollo down the noisy streets.

He turns about to face the loud uproar
And drives the rebels to their very door.
The frequent stone is hurled where'er they go;
When badgers fight, then every one's a foe.
The dogs are clapt and urged to join the fray;
The badger turns and drives them all away.
Though scarcely half as big, demure and small,
He fights with dogs for hours and beats them all.
The heavy mastiff, savage in the fray,
Lies down and licks his feet and turns away.
The bulldog knows his match and waxes cold.
The badger grins and never leaves his hold.
He drives the crowd and follows at their heels
And bites them through – the drunkard swears and reels.

The frightened women take the boys away,
The blackguard laughs and hurries on the fray.
He tries to reach the woods, an awkward race,
But sticks and cudgels quickly stop the chase.
He turns agen and drives the noisy crowd
And beats the many dogs in noises loud.
He drives away and beats them every one,
And then they loose them all and set them on.
He falls as dead and kicked by boys and men,
Then starts and grins and drives the crowd agen;
Till kicked and torn and beaten out he lies
And leaves his hold and cackles, groans and dies.

JOHN CLARE

The Ghost Heath Run

JOHN MASEFIELD

This is a small part of a very long poem. It starts at a trot, breaks into a marvellous gallop, and then pants to a conclusion of tired horses, exhausted but jubilant riders, and the fox at his last choking gasp. It is both exciting and terrible, sad and funny. It goes on for hundreds and hundreds of lines, of which never a one seems anything but essential.

*

The fox knew well as he ran the dark,
That the headlong hounds were past their mark;
They had missed his swerve and had overrun,
But their devilish play was not yet done.

149

For a minute he ran and heard no sound,
Then a whimper came from a questing hound,
Then a 'This way, beauties,' and then 'Leu, Leu,'
The floating laugh of the horn that blew.
Then the cry again, and the crash and rattle
Of the shrubs burst back as they ran to battle,
Till the wood behind seemed risen from root,
Crying and crashing, to give pursuit,
Till the trees seemed hounds and the air seemed cry,
And the earth so far that he needs must die,
Die where he reeled in the woodland dim,
With a hound's white grips in the spine of him.
For one more burst he could spurt, and then
Wait for the teeth, and the wrench, and men.

He made his spurt for the Mourne End rocks,
The air blew rank with the taint of fox;
The yews gave way to a greener space
Of great stone strewn in a grassy place.
And there was his earth at the great grey shoulder
Sunk in the ground, of a granite boulder.
A dry, deep burrow with rocky roof,
Proof against crowbars, terrier proof,
Life to the dying, rest for bones.

The earth was stopped; it was filled with stones.

Then for a moment his courage failed,
His eyes looked up as his body quailed,
Then the coming of death, which all things dread,
Made him run for the wood ahead.

The taint of fox was rank on the air,
He knew, as he ran, there were foxes there.
His strength was broken, his heart was bursting,
His bones were rotten, his throat was thirsting;
His feet were reeling, his brush was thick
From dragging the mud, and his brain was sick.

He thought as he ran of his old delight
In the wood in the moon in an April night,
His happy hunting, his winter loving,
The smells of things in the midnight roving,
The look of his dainty-nosing, red,
Clean-felled dam with her footpad's tread;
Of his sire, so swift, so game, so cunning,
With craft in his brain and power of running;
Their fights of old when his teeth drew blood;
Now he was sick, with his coat all mud.

He crossed the covert, he crawled the bank,
To a meuse in the thorns, and there he sank,
With his ears flexed back and his teeth shown white
In a rat's resolve for a dying bite.

And there, as he lay, he saw the vale,
That a struggling sunlight silvered pale:
The Deerlip Brook like a strip of steel,
The Nun's Wood Yews where the rabbits squeal,
The great grass square of the Roman Fort,
And the smoke in the elms at Crendon Court.

And above the smoke in the elm-tree tops
Was the beech-clump's blur, Blown Hilcote Copse,
Where he and his mates had long made merry
In the bloody joys of the rabbit-herry.

And there as he lay and looked, the cry
Of the hounds at head came rousing by;
He bent his bones in the blackthorn dim.

But the cry of the hounds was not for him.
Over the fence with a crash they went,
Belly to grass, with a burning scent;
Then came Dansey, yelling to Bob:
'They've changed! Oh, damn it! now here's a job.'
And Bob yelled back: 'Well, we cannot turn 'em;
It's Jumper and Antic, Tom, we'll learn 'em!
We must just go on, and hope we kill.'
They followed hounds down the Mourne End Hill.

The fox lay still in the rabbit-meuse,
On the dry brown dust of the plumes of yews.
In the bottom below a brook went by,
Blue, in a patch, like a streak of sky.
There one by one, with a clink of stone,
Came a red or dark coat on a horse half-blown.
And man to man with a gasp for breath
Said: 'Lord, what a run! I'm fagged to death.'

After an hour no riders came,
The day drew by like an ending game;
A robin sang from a pufft red breast,
The fox lay quiet and took his rest.
A wren on a tree-stump carolled clear,
Then the starlings wheeled in a sudden sheer,
The rooks came home to the twiggy hive
In the elm-tree tops which the winds do drive.
Then the noise of the rooks fell slowly still,
And the lights came out in the Clench Brook Mill;

Then a pheasant cocked, then an owl began,
With a cry that curdles the blood of man.

The stars grew bright as the yews grew black,
The fox rose stiffly and stretched his back,
He flaired the air, then he padded out
To the valley below him, dark as doubt,
Winter-thin with the young green crops,
For old Cold Crendon and Hilcote Copse.
As he crossed the meadows at Naunton Larking
The dogs in the town all started barking,
For with feet all bloody and flanks all foam,
The hounds and the hunt were limping home;
Limping home in the dark dead-beaten,
The hounds all rank from a fox they'd eaten.
Dansey saying to Robin Dawe:
'The fastest and longest I ever saw.'
And Robin answered: 'Oh, Tom, 'twere good!
I thought they'd changed in the Mourne End Wood,
But now I feel that they did not change.
We've had a run that was great and strange;
And to kill in the end, at dusk, on grass!
We'll turn to the Cock and take a glass,
For hounds, poor souls! are past their forces;
And a gallon of ale for our poor horses,
And some bits of bread for the hounds, poor things!
After all they've done (for they've done like kings)
Would keep them going till we get in.
We had it alone from Nun's Wood Whin.'
Then Tom replied: 'If they changed or not,
There've been few runs longer and none more hot;
We shall talk of today until we die.'

The stars grew bright in the winter sky,
The wind came keen with a tang of frost,
The brook was troubled for new things lost,
The copse was happy for old things found,
The fox came home and he went to ground.

(from *Reynard the Fox*, 1919)

153

A Runnable Stag

When the pods went pop on the broom, green broom,
  And apples began to be golden-skinned,
We harboured a stag in the Priory coomb,
  And we feathered his trail up-wind, up-wind,
  We feathered his trail up-wind –
    A stag of warrant,* a stag, a stag,
    A runnable stag, a kingly crop,
    Brow, bay and tray and three on top,
    A stag, a runnable stag.

Then the huntsman's horn rang yap, yap, yap,
  And 'Forwards' we heard the harbourer shout;
But 'twas only a brocket that broke a gap
  In the beechen underwood, driven out,
  From the underwood antlered out
    By warrant and might of the stag, the stag,
    The runnable stag, whose lordly mind
    Was bent on sleep, though beamed and tined
    He stood, a runnable stag.

So we tufted the covert till afternoon
  With Tinkerman's Pup and Bell-of-the-North;
And hunters were sulky and hounds out of tune
  Before we tufted the right stag forth,
  Before we tufted him forth,
    The stag of warrant, the wily stag,
    The runnable stag with his kingly crop,
    Brow, bay and tray and three on top,
    The royal and runnable stag.

* 'A stag of warrant' is one that is ready to be killed for venison.

It was Bell-of-the-North and Tinkerman's Pup
That stuck to the scent till the copse was drawn.
'Tally ho! tally ho!' and the hunt was up,
The tufters whipped and the pack laid on
The resolute pack laid on,
And the stag of warrant away at last,
The runnable stag, the same, the same,
His hoofs on fire, his horns like flame,
A stag, a runnable stag.

'Let your gelding be: if you check or chide
He stumbles at once and you're out of the hunt;
For three hundred gentlemen, able to ride,
On hunters accustomed to bear the brunt,
Accustomed to bear the brunt,
Are after the runnable stag, the stag,
The runnable stag with his kingly crop,
Brow, bay and tray and three on top,
The right, the runnable stag.'

By perilous paths in coomb and dell,
The heather, the rocks, and the river-bed,
The pace grew hot, for the scent lay well,
And a runnable stag goes right ahead,
The quarry went right ahead —
Ahead, ahead, and fast and far;
His antlered crest, his cloven hoof,
Brow, bay and tray and three aloof,
The stag, the runnable stag.

For a matter of twenty miles and more,
By the densest hedge and the highest wall,
Through herds of bullocks he baffled the lore
Of harbourer, huntsman, hounds and all,
Of harbourer, hounds and all —
The stag of warrant, the wily stag,
For twenty miles, and five and five,
He ran and he never was caught alive,
This stag, this runnable stag.

When he turned at bay in the leafy gloom,
   In the emerald gloom where the brook ran deep,
He heard in the distance the rollers boom,
   And he saw in a vision of peaceful sleep,
   In a wonderful vision of sleep,
     A stag of warrant, a stag, a stag,
     A runnable stag in a jewelled bed,
     Under the sheltering ocean dead,
     A stag, a runnable stag.

So a fateful hope lit up his eye,
   And he opened his nostrils wide again,
And he tossed his branching antlers high
   As he headed the hunt down the Charlock glen,
   As he raced down the echoing glen
     For five miles more, the stag, the stag,
     For twenty miles, and five and five,
     Not to be caught now, dead or alive,
     The stag, the runnable stag.

Three hundred gentlemen, able to ride,
   Three hundred horses as gallant and free,
Beheld him escape on the evening tide,
   Far out till he sank in the Severn Sea,
   Till he sank in the depths of the sea —
     The stag, the buoyant stag, the stag
     That slept at last in a jewelled bed
     Under the sheltering ocean spread,
     The stag, the runnable stag.

JOHN DAVIDSON

Tarka the Otter

HENRY WILLIAMSON

Meanwhile Tarka, swimming out of the sycamore holt, had turned to deeper water and gone under the railway bridge twenty yards below – the line with its embankment and three bridges cut the S from south to north. He kept close to the left bank, in the margin of shade. The copse ended at the bridge; below was a meadow. He rose to breathe, heard hounds, and swam on underwater. He passed a run of peal, which flashed aside when they saw him and sped above the bridge at many times the pace of a travelling otter. Sixty yards below the bridge, by the roots of a thrown alder, Tarka rose to listen. Looking around, he saw neither hound nor man, and knew that he was not being followed. He thought of the holt under the oak tree above the next railway bridge, and swam on down.

Where the river's bend began to straighten again, the right bank lay under oak trees growing on the hill-slope to the sky. Tarka dived and swam across the river to the holt he had remembered as he left the roots of the sycamore. This holt had a sunken opening, where no terrier could enter. Here Tarka's sire had been asleep when hounds had found him two years before. Tarka swung up, coming into a dark cavern lit by a small hole above, and stinking of paraffin poured there the previous afternoon. He sniffed the oil film on the water, and turned back into the weir-pool.

Again he made a hidden crossing, to listen under cover of flag-lilies for more than a minute. The river was quiet. He heard the sound of falling water, and swam slowly down, after touching under the bank. He passed under the middle arch of the railway bridge, and reached the weir slanting across the river. The summer water tumbled down the fish-pass, but glided thin as a snail's shell over the top end of the concrete sill. The lower end by the fender at the head of the leat was dry. Tarka walked along the sill, nearly to the end, which was two inches above the level of the pool. He stretched his weary back on the warm concrete and sprawled in the sun.

He lay basking for more than an hour, enjoying the sound of water tumbling in the pass and sliding down the face of the weir. Swallows dipped in the pool, and sometimes a peal leapt in the shadow of the bridge. Tarka's head was always raised before the fish fell back, but he did not leave the sill. Warm and brilliant sun-flickers on the shadows below dazed his eyes, and made him drowsy, but when a hound, working along down the left bank, climbed on the sill by the pass and shook himself, he was instantly alert. Half lying down, he remained quite still, while the hound lifted its muzzle to sniff. Something moved on the bridge – otter and hound turned their heads together, seeing a man behind the railing. At first the man saw only the hound, but when it walked along the sill and ran down the face of the weir, he saw the otter it was following. The man had come along the railway to see if many fish were in the pool; he was a poacher nick-named Shiner, and the top of one of his fingers was missing. He had no love for otters. Along the railway line he hastened, and shouted to the otter-hunters.

Followed in silence by the hound Pitiful, Tarka swam leisurely. He watched, from under a tree, a single enemy working down the shallow, crossing a deeper water to seek his scent along the banks. He let it come within a few feet of his head, then dived and swam away. Pitiful never saw him, or the chain of bubbles. Often she followed the wash carried down with the current; and when it grew weak, she would amble along the banks until she found where the otter had touched.

Tarka felt neither fear nor rage against the hound. He wanted to be left alone. After several hidden swims from bank to bank, and finding no holding where he might lie up and sleep until evening, he walked out by a cattle-trodden grove in the right bank, and ran away over land. He followed the otter-path across a quarter of a mile of meadow, and came to the river again by the third oak above Canal Bridge.

Tarka drifted under the high lime-spiky arches of the

158

bridge, and the white owl, roosting on a ledge below the parapet, beside the briars of a dog-rose growing there with hawkweeds, saw him going downstream.

Bees came to the wild roses, crammed more pollen into their laden thigh-bags, and burred away over the bridge. A petal dropped, a swallow played with it as it fell, clipping it with first one wing and then the other, until it dropped into the water, and was carried away, past the gap in the bank where the Owlery Oak, Tarka's birth-place, had been held by its roots two years before.

Then Pitiful swam under the Canal Bridge, and after her the pack came down, and many men, and the owl was driven into wavy flight down the river. It pitched in the tree of Leaning Willow Island, as a dull clamour broke out half a mile up the river. Hounds had marked the otter under a hover, and driven him out.

The water of the pool was swimming deep from the shallow above Canal Bridge to the shallow above Leaning Willow Island. The surface above Tarka mirrored the bed of the river – the dark rocks, the weed, the sodden branches, with the legs and bodies of hounds – until ripples broke the mirror into shades of light. In this underwater realm, where sounds were so distinct – the crush of nailed boots on stones, the tip-tap of poles, the thresh of hounds' legs, and even the flip of cyclops and waterflea – Tarka swam until he was forced to vent, which he did at the river verge, under the banks, or by clumps of yellow flags. Sometimes he crept on the stones, hiding himself under overhanging roots as he sought a refuge, until dreading the nearness of hounds he slipped into the river again, covered with a silver skin of air. As he swam, twin streams of bubbles came out of his nostrils, raced over his head and neck, and shook off his back to lie on the surface in a chain, watched by many eyes. Up and down the pool he went, swimming in midstream or near the banks, crossing from side to side and varying his depth of swimming as he tried to get away from his pursuers. Passing under the legs of hounds, he saw them joined to their broken surface-images. From underwater he saw men and women, pointing with hand and pole, at palsied and distorted shapes on the bank. However hard he swam with his three and a half webs, always he heard the hounds, as they spoke to his scent lying in burst bubble, in seal on muddy scour, on leaf and twig. Once in mid-river, while on his way to a clump of flags, his breath gave out, and he bobbed up to breathe a yard from Deadlock. He stared into the eyes of his old enemy; and dived. During forty seconds, he swam a distance of seventy yards, to a bed of reeds, where he breathed and rested. No one saw him; but they saw the chain.

Up the river again, past the Peal Rock, and under the middle arch of Canal Bridge to the shallow, crossed by a line of men and women, white and blue and green and red and grey, standing close together.

Tally-Ho!

He turned and reached covering water just before hounds.

'Get onto'm! Leu-on! leu-on! Wind him, old fellars!' The huntsman was wading up to his waist in the water, scooping the air with his grey hat. Bellman, a small-footed hairy black and tan, cross between a drafted harrier and a Dumfries-shire rough otter-hound, yelped his impatience, seeming to snap the water as he swam. Sometimes the huntsman gave an encouraging spit-note on his horn. Tarka went down-river, but a blurred and brilliant colour band stretched from bank to bank above Leaning Willow Island. He tried to get through the stickle, but stocking'd leg was pressed to stocking'd leg, a fixed barrier behind plying poles. The owl flew out of the willow, miserable in the sunlight with small birds pursuing it.

Tarka turned and swam upstream again, leaving hounds behind. For five minutes he rested under a thorn bush. Deadlock found him, and on he went, to Canal Bridge once more, where he lay in the water, weary after a long chase. At the beginning of the sixth hour he tried to pass the higher stickle, but his enemies stood firm on the stones. The tongues swelled under the bridge. He was nearly picked up by Hurricane, the Irish staghound, but the blunted canine teeth could not hold him.

The chain became shorter. Tarka was too weary to seek a holding in the banks. He breathed in view of his enemies. Seven and a half couples of hounds swam in the pool, their sterns throwing behind them arc-lines of drops on the surface. Others splashed in the shallows under the banks. The huntsman let them work by themselves.

During the sixth hour the otter disappeared. The river grew quiet. People not in uniform sat down on the grass. The huntsman was wading slowly upstream, feeling foot-hold with pole and keeping an eye on Deadlock. Stickle stood slack, but ready to bar the way with pole-strokes. Look-outs gazed at the water before them. It was known that the otter might leave the river at any moment. The boy with the warped pole, on whose cheeks were two patches of dried otter-blood, was already opening his knife, ready to cut another notch on the handle in the form of a cross.

But for more than an hour the sun-thongs flickered across the placid water; and in softening light the owl returned, flying high over the bridge, to the mouse runs in the quiet meadow beyond.

A fallen bough of willow lay in the pool near one bank, and Tarka lay beside it. His rudder held a sunken branch. Only his wide upper nostrils were above the water. He never moved. Every yard of the banks between the stickles was searched again. Poles were thrust into branches, roots, and clumps of flag-lilies. The wading huntsman prodded Peal

161

Rock and the rock above it. Hounds sat on the banks, shivering, and watching Deadlock, Render, and Harper working the banks. The crack of a whip, a harsh voice rating – Rufus had turned a rabbit out of a bramble and was chasing it across the meadow. He returned to the river in a wide circle, eyeing the whip.

At the beginning of the eighth hour a scarlet dragonfly whirred and darted over the willow snag, watched by a girl sitting on the bank. Her father, an old man lank and humped as a heron, was looking out near her. She watched the dragonfly settle on what looked like a piece of bark beside the snag; she heard a sneeze, and saw the otter's whiskers scratch the water. Glancing round, she realized that she alone had seen the otter. She flushed, and hid her grey eyes with her lashes. Since childhood she had walked the Devon rivers with her father, looking for flowers and the nests of birds, passing rocks and trees as old friends, seeing a Spirit everywhere, gentle in thought to all her eyes beheld.

For two minutes the maid sat silent, hardly daring to look at the river. The dragonfly flew over the pool, seizing flies and tearing them apart in its horny jaws. Her father watched it as it settled on the snag, rose up, circled, and lit on the water, it seemed. Tarka sneezed again, and the dragonfly flew away. A grunt of satisfaction from the old man, a brown hand and wrist holding a lot of hat, a slow intake breath, and,

Tally-Ho!

Tarka dived when the hounds came down, and the chain showed where he had swum. Many saw his dark sleek form as he walked by the edge of a grassy islet by the twelve trees. The hounds ran to him, and Tarka turned and faced them, squatting on his short hindlegs, his paws close against his round and sturdy chest. He bit Render in the nose, making his teeth meet. In an instant he drew back, hissing, and bit Deadlock in the flews. The narrow lower jaw snapped again and again, until the press of hounds hid him from sight.

He squirmed away through legs and under bellies, biting and writhing a way to the water; and the chain drew out on the surface of the pool while hounds were still seeking him on the stones where he had sat and faced them.

Leu-on, then! Leu-on! Ov-ov-ov-ov-over!

Tarka's pace was slow and his dives were short. In the water by the Peal Rock he lay, glancing at the faces along the banks, across the river, and in the river. His small dark eyes showed no feeling. He turned away from the human faces, to watch the coming of the hounds. He was calm and fearless and fatigued. When they were his length away, he swung under, showing the middle of his smooth back level with the surface, and swimming past their legs. He saw the huntsman's legs before him joined to the image of legs, and above the inverted image a flattened and uncertain head and shoulders. Up and down he swam, slower and slower.

At the beginning of the ninth hour an immense fatigue came over him, greater than his fatigue when in the long hard winter he had lived for over a month on seaweed and shellfish in the estuary. He was swimming up from the lower stickle when the water seemed to thicken at each thrust of his webs. He ceased to swim and drifted backwards. Barbrook touched his neck as he dived. He reappeared two poles' length away, and lay still, looking at the huntsman wading nearer.

For ten minutes he rested, between dives of a few yards only, and then rolled from Deadlock's bite and went downstream. He swam with his last strength, for upon him had come the penultimate desire of the hunted otter, the desire that comes when the water ceases to be a refuge, the desire to tread again the land-tracks of his ancestors. He crawled half up the bank, but turned back at the thudding of many feet, and swam down to the stickle. The sideway ply of a pole in a turmoil of water struck him on the head. He pushed past the iron point, but it was brought down on his shoulder, to hold him against the shillets. Hounds were fifteen yards away, urged on by hat and horn and the yarring cheers of the whippers-in. Thrice Tarka's teeth clicked on the iron pressing his shoulder as he strove against the weight of the sportsman trying to lift him back. A second pole was brought down from the other flank, crossing with the first. The wooden pincers held him; he twisted like an eel and bit into a leg. With furious strength he writhed from the crossed poles, and through the stickle, as Deadlock bore down upon him and pulled him back by the rudder. Amidst the harsh cries of men

163

and women and the heavy tongues of hounds Tarka was overborne by the pack. The Master looked at his watch – eight hours and forty-five minutes from the find in Dark Pool. The screeching, yarring yell of one of the honorary whips: Yaa-aa-ee-io! Leu-in on 'm! Yaa-ee-oo! for again Tarka had escaped from the worry, and had merged into the narrow stream of water that hurried to Leaning Willow Island.

Below the island the river widened, smooth with the sky. Tarka swam down slowly, bleeding from many wounds. Sometimes he paddled with three legs, sometimes with one, in the water darkening so strangely before his eyes. Not always did he hear the hounds baying around him. At the beginning of the tenth hour he passed the banks faced with stone to keep the sea from the village, and drifted into deeper water, whereon sticks and froth were floating. Hounds were called off by the horn, for the tide was at flood.

But as they were about to leave, Tarka was seen again, moving with the tide, his mouth open. The flow took him near the bank; he kicked feebly, and rolled over.

Tally-Ho!

Deadlock saw the small brown head, and bayed in triumph as he jumped down the bank. He bit the head, and lifted the otter high, flung him about and fell into the water with him. They saw the broken head look up beside Deadlock, heard the cry of Ic-yang! as Tarka bit into his throat, and the hound was sinking with the otter into the deep water. Oak leaves, black and rotting in the mud of the unseen bed, arose and swirled and sank again. And the tide slowed still, and began to move back, and they waited and watched, until the body of Deadlock arose, drowned and heavy, and floated away amidst the froth on the waters.

They pulled the body out of the river and carried it to the bank, laying it on the grass, and looking down at the dead hound in sad wonder. And while they stood there silently, a great bubble rose out of the depths, and broke, and as they watched, another bubble shook the surface, and broke; and there was a third bubble in the sea-going waters, and nothing more.

(from Tarka the Otter, 1927)

PEOPLE

Anthony Crundle

Here lies the body of
ANTHONY CRUNDLE
Farmer, of this parish,
Who died in 1849 at the age of 82.
'He delighted in music.'

R.I.P.

And of
SUSAN

For fifty-three years his wife
Who died in 1860, aged 86.

Anthony Crundle of Dorrington Wood
　Played on a piccolo. Lord was he,
For seventy years, of sheaves that stood
　Under the perry and cider tree;
　Anthony Crundle, R.I.P.

And because he prospered with sickle and scythe,
　With cattle afield and labouring ewe,
Anthony was uncommonly blithe,
　And played of a night to himself and Sue.
　Anthony Crundle, eighty-two.

The earth to till, and a tune to play,
　And Susan for fifty years and three,
And Dorrington Wood at the end of the day . . .
　May providence do no worse by me;
　Anthony Crundle, R.I.P.

JOHN DRINKWATER

Nottingham and the Mining Country

D. H. LAWRENCE

The novelist D. H. Lawrence was a miner's son from Nottinghamshire who spent much of his adult life abroad. Here he looks back at the countryside and its way of life, fast disappearing, that he once knew.

*

I was born nearly forty-four years ago, in Eastwood, a mining village of some three thousand souls, about eight miles from Nottingham, and one mile from a small stream, the Erewash, which divides Nottinghamshire from Derbyshire. It is hilly country, looking west to Crich and towards Matlock, sixteen miles away, and east and north-east towards Mansfield and the Sherwood Forest district. To me it seemed, and still seems, an extremely beautiful countryside, just between the red sandstone and the oak-trees of Nottingham, and the cold limestone, the ash-trees, the stone fences of Derbyshire. To me, as a child and a young man, it was still the old England of the forest and agricultural past; there were no motor-cars, the mines were, in a sense, an accident in the landscape, and Robin Hood and his merry men were not very far away.

The string of coal-mines of B. W. & Co. had been opened some sixty years before I was born, and Eastwood had come into being as a consequence. It must have been a tiny village at the beginning of the nineteenth century, a small place of cottages and fragmentary rows of little four-roomed miners' dwellings, the homes of the old colliers of the eighteenth century, who worked in the bits of mines, foot-hill mines with an opening in the hillside into which the miners walked, or windlass mines, where the men were wound up one at a

167

time, in a bucket, by a donkey. The windlass mines were still working when my father was a boy – and the shafts of some were still there, when I was a boy.

But somewhere about 1820 the company must have sunk the first big shaft – not very deep – and installed the first machinery of the real industrial colliery. Then came my grandfather, a young man trained to be a tailor, drifting from the south of England, and got the job of company tailor for the Brinsley mine. In those days the company supplied the men with the thick flannel vests, or singlets, and the moleskin trousers lined at the top with flannel, in which the colliers worked. I remember the great rolls of coarse flannel and pit-cloth which stood in the corner of my grandfather's shop when I was a small boy, and the big, strange old sewing-machine, like nothing else on earth, which sewed the massive pit-trousers. But when I was only a child the company discontinued supplying the men with pit-clothes.

My grandfather settled in an old cottage down in a quarry-bed, by the brook at Old Brinsley, near the pit. A mile away, up at Eastwood, the company built the first miners' dwellings – it must be nearly a hundred years ago. Now Eastwood occupies a lovely position on a hilltop, with the steep slope towards Derbyshire and the long slope towards Nottingham. They put up a new church, which stands fine and commanding, even if it has no real form, looking across the awful Erewash Valley at the church of Heanor, similarly commanding, away on a hill beyond. What opportunities, what opportunities! These mining villages *might* have been like the lovely hill-towns of Italy, shapely and fascinating. And what happened?

Most of the little rows of dwellings of the old-style miners were pulled down, and dull little shops began to rise along the Nottingham Road, while on the down-slope of the north side the company erected what is still known as the New Buildings, or the Square. These New Buildings consist of two great hollow squares of dwellings planked down on the rough slope of the hill, little four-room houses with the 'front' looking outward into the grim, blank street, and the 'back', with a tiny square brick yard, a low wall, and a w.c. and ash pit, looking into the desert of the square, hard, uneven, jolting black earth tilting rather steeply down, with these little back yards all round, and opening at the corners. The squares were quite big, and absolutely desert, save for the posts for clothes lines, and people passing, children playing on the hard earth. And they were shut in like a barracks enclosure, very strange.

Even fifty years ago the squares were unpopular. It was 'common' to live in the Square. It was a little less common to live in the Breach, which consisted of six blocks of rather more pretentious dwellings erected by the company in the valley below, two rows of three blocks, with an alley between. And it was most 'common', most degraded of all to live in Dakins Row, two rows of the old dwellings, very old, black four-roomed little places, that stood on the hill again, not far from the Square.

So the place started. Down the steep street between the squares, Scargill Street, the Wesleyans' chapel was put up, and I was born in the little corner shop just above. Across the other side of the Square the miners themselves built the big, barn-like Primitive Methodist chapel. Along the hill-top ran the Nottingham Road, with its scrappy, ugly mid-Victorian shops. The little market-place, with a superb outlook, ended the village on the Derbyshire side, and was just here left bare with the Sun Inn on one side, the chemist across, with the gilt pestle-and-mortar, and a shop at the other corner, the corner of Alfreton Road and Nottingham Road.

In this queer jumble of the old England and the new, I came into consciousness. As I remember, little local speculators already began to straggle dwellings in rows, always in rows, across the fields: nasty red-brick, flat-faced dwellings with dark slate roofs. The bay-window period only began when I was a child. But most of the country was untouched.

There must be three or four hundred company houses in the squares and the streets that surround the squares, like a great barracks wall. There must be sixty or eighty company houses in the Breach. The old Dakins Row will have thirty to forty little holes. Then counting the old cottages and rows left with their old gardens down the lanes and along the twitchells, and even in the midst of Nottingham Road itself, there were houses enough for the population, there was no need for much building. And not much building went on when I was small.

We lived in the Breach, in a corner house. A field-path came down under a great hawthorn hedge. On the other side was the brook, with the old sheep-bridge going over into the meadows. The hawthorn hedge by the brook had grown tall as tall trees, and we used to bathe from there in the dipping-hole, where the sheep were dipped, just near the fall from the old mill-dam, where the water rushed. The mill only ceased grinding the local corn when I was a child. And my father, who always worked in Brinsley pit, and who always got up at five o'clock, if not at four, would set off in the dawn across the fields at Coney Grey, and hunt for mushrooms in the long grass, or perhaps pick up a skulking rabbit, which he would bring home at evening inside the lining of his pit-coat.

So that the life was a curious cross between industrialism and the old agricultural England of Shakespeare and Milton and Fielding and George Eliot.

(from 'Nottingham and the Mining Country', 1936)

170

The Good Spirit of Sherwood

ROGER LANCELYN GREEN

The legendary figure we know as Robin Hood appears in many and many an ancient ballad. A Little Geste of Robin Hood and his Meiny *is the one most often found. It is full of old unfamiliar words –* meiny *can be translated* company *or* retinue, *what we call more familiarly his* merry men. *The old ballads go on and on, as ballads must; so perhaps it is best to come to Robin through translation into prose –* Roger Lancelyn Green *has done a good job here, for his simple, straightforward writing does approximate in some way to the flat open rhythm of the ballads:*

> In somer when the shawes be sheyne,
>   And leves be large and long,
> Hit is full mery in feyre foreste
>   To here the foulys song:
>
> To se the dere draw to the dale,
>   And leve the hillès hee,
> And shadow hem in the levës grene,
>   Under the grene-wode tre . . .
>
> Hit befel on Whitsontide,
>   Erly in a May mornyng . . .
>   *and so on . . .*

*

1

Sherwood in the twilight, is Robin Hood awake?
Grey and ghostly shadows are gliding through the brake,
Shadows of the dappled deer, dreaming of the morn,
Dreaming of a shadowy man that winds a shadowy horn

ALFRED NOYES: *Sherwood* (1903)

171

King Richard The First, Richard Coeur de Lion, came to the throne in 1189 – and very soon left his throne empty when he set off on the Crusade to free Jerusalem from the Saracens. He was summoned home by the news of trouble and rebellion – but was captured on the way and shut up in a prison – and in England few believed that he would ever return.

When he went away, Richard left the Bishop of Ely to rule for him, but very soon the King's wicked brother, Prince John, accused the Bishop of treason, and made him fly for his life, and himself became ruler of the country.

John was a cruel, merciless man, and most of his followers were as bad as he. They needed money, and he needed money: the easiest way of getting it was to accuse some wealthy man of treason or law-breaking, make him an outlaw – and seize his house or castle and all his goods. For an outlaw could own nothing, and anyone who killed him would be rewarded.

When Prince John had seized a man's lands he would usually put one of his followers in his place – provided he paid him large sums of money. Prince John's followers did not mind how they came by this money: for them the easiest way was to take it from the small farmers, the peasants and even from the serfs. And not only Prince John's upstart knights and squires did this, but many also of the Bishops and Abbots who were either in league with him, or greedy for their own good like the worst of the nobles and barons.

Many a Sheriff, too, was appointed to keep order and administer justice in the towns and counties by Prince John – provided he paid well for the honour: and of course he had also to force the money from someone weaker than himself, and obey Prince John however cruel and unjust his orders might be.

Such a one was the Sheriff of Nottingham, the little town on the edge of Sherwood Forest, and when Prince John came and set up his Court there for a time, he was naturally most eager to show his loyalty and zeal.

One evening he and his men came upon a serf who had killed a deer. Without a thought of pity, the Sheriff ordered the poor man's cottage to be searched for money, and when none was found, had it burnt to the ground.

Then the wretched serf was brought before him.

'You know the Forest Laws,' said the Sheriff grimly. 'All right, my men: one of you heat the irons quickly. Blind him, and turn him loose!'

'No, no! Not that!' shrieked the man. 'Anything but that! Kill me straightaway! If you blind me, God will repay you! Mercy! Mercy!'

Prince John had ridden out to see the Sheriff at work, and at this moment he joined the little group round the glowing embers of the cottage.

'What nightjar have we here?' he asked carelessly. 'Surely, good Sheriff, you should have cut out his tongue first. You should keep silent and secret if you expect this bogey Robin Hood to come to his aid, as I've heard tell he does. Why, this man's cries will waken the King in Palestine, or wherever he is now!'

'Silence, you dog!' cried the Sheriff, striking the serf roughly across the mouth. 'You ought to know better than to make this unseemly noise in the presence of His Royal Highness Prince John!'

'Prince John! Prince John!' gasped the man. 'Oh, save me, sire! For God's love, save me!'

'Who is he?' asked John casually. 'What has he done?'

'They call him Much,' said the Sheriff importantly. 'He was a miller once. But he was too fond of the King's deer. See, his first and second fingers have been cut off: that tells its own story – a bowstring pulled unlawfully. Now we've caught him at it again: the law lays it down that for a second conviction for deer-slaying, a man shall have his eyes burnt out. A third time – and he hangs. But I'll warrant he'll find it hard to shoot a deer when we've done with him: I've never known a man to shoot by smell – ha! ha!'

The Sheriff laughed heartily at his own joke, and Prince John was pleased to smile.

'Well, fellow?' he said to poor old Much, who still knelt trembling before him.

'So please your highness,' gasped Much, 'they burnt my

mill to make a wider hunting-ground and a way to the stream
so that the deer could come there to drink. How could I get
my food but by hunting? It's hard to shoot straight and true
lacking the arrow fingers, and true and straight must a man
shoot if he would kill lawful game, the rabbit and the wood-
pigeon . . . I had two children, one died of want, and my boy,
young Much, was crying out for food . . . We cannot live
long upon grass and herbs like an ox, nor upon roots that the
swine eat.'

'Oh,' said Prince John, 'so you decided to try a richer diet,
did you! The king's deer! . . . Was there no other way? No,
no, Master Sheriff, let me deal justly with him . . . What of
this Robin Hood of whom tales are told? Some rich man, they
say – a yeoman or a nobleman born of some old Saxon family
– who, mad fool, brings help to such dirt as you and your kin
of law breakers, kills the king's deer himself, and has even
robbed a purse on the highway before now . . . Well, where
is he? And, more to the point, W H O is he? Tell me that, and
you shall keep your eyes – to see your way to the gallows one
day, I'll be bound!'

'I know not who he is!' gasped Much. 'Robin Hood comes
out of the forest – men say he is the Good Spirit of Sherwood
– and having brought help, he goes away as silently as he
came. No one has seen him by daylight . . .'

'Faugh!' cried Prince John impatiently. 'Take him away
and do your work on him out of my sight. These rogues are
too loyal for my liking, or for their own good.'

So four of the Sheriff's men dragged poor Much away
while a fifth drew the glowing irons from the fire which had
been his home and followed grimly at his heels. But suddenly
with a desperate cry he tore himself loose, snatched a sword
from one of them, and made a rush at Prince John. He never
reached him, however, for with a sudden vicious whine an
arrow sped from behind them and laid him dead on the
ground.

'A good shot, truly,' remarked Prince John, 'though I
could wish that it had but maimed him. A dead man is no
bait for this Robin Hood . . . Who was it loosed this arrow?'

He turned as he spoke, and saw advancing towards him

from the edge of the glade a short dark man wearing a green cloak over his suit of brown leather.

'My lord,' said the man, bowing very low before Prince John, 'I am called Worman, Steward to Robert Fitzooth, Earl of Huntingdon.'

Prince John's smile twisted itself suddenly into a scowl of anger.

'Earl of Huntingdon, indeed!' he exclaimed, 'I have heard tell of this nonsense before – David Lord Carrick is the Earl – Northumberland's son. What pretence is this?'

'Pardon me, my lord,' protested Worman, cringing before Prince John. 'Hereabouts men call Fitzooth Earl of Huntingdon, by right of his mother and the Saxon line of the old Earls. He is my master, so I dare not call him otherwise!'

Prince John nodded. 'I would know more of this supposed Earl,' he said in his most cruel and silky tones. 'Is he loyal, think you?'

'To King Richard – yes,' answered Worman with meaning in his voice.

'Richard – Richard – everywhere Richard!' snarled John. 'Richard is dead – or as good as dead – rotting in some dungeon. That mad minstrel Blondel will never find him! I am King: King in all but name . . . This fellow Fitzooth: is he rich? Are his lands wide?'

'Once they were wide indeed,' said Worman, 'but now only the house and lands of Locksley remain to him. The other lands he has sold.'

'Ha, then his coffers must be full of gold!' cried Prince John.

'Even I his Steward do not know that,' answered Worman. 'I know only that he has some secret need for money, though what it is he keeps to himself and no one in his household knows except his friend and body-servant William Scathlock.'

'How could I see him unknown?' mused Prince John. 'If I heard but a word of treason – well, we would see what was in those coffers . . . And you, my good fellow, should have your pickings – if you prove true and secret.'

'Against my master?' said Worman. 'Can I betray him? But indeed my duty to you, sire, overweights all other duties . . . Then I will tell you how it can be done. Tomorrow Earl Robert is to be married at Fountains Abbey to the Lady Marian, daughter of Lord Fitzwalter. Tonight he holds a great feast in his own great house of Locksley Hall: all guests will be welcome and no close watch kept as to who they are. If you and the Sheriff come disguised – as palmers from the Holy Land, perhaps, with some tall tale of King Richard – you will have a ready welcome.'

'I like the scheme,' exclaimed Prince John who, for all his faults, never lacked courage. 'Come with me, good fellow; and you, Master Sheriff, gather your men and come also: we have little time to waste. Leave that dead dog there – as a warning to Robin Hood should he come this way.'

When they had ridden off into the grey of the evening, and silence had fallen upon Sherwood once again, certain bent and maimed figures began to creep out of the near-by thickets and gather round the body of old Much the miller which lay where it had fallen near the still smoking ashes of his home.

'He's dead,' exclaimed one of them. 'Well, better than blinding . . . These are cruel times.'

'Aye,' cried another, 'but when the King comes home from the Crusade, things will be better.'

'But if he never comes back,' muttered a third, 'then that devil Prince John will be King – and God have mercy on us then.'

'Here's that poor lad Much, son of the man they've murdered,' interrupted another. 'What can we do for him? The old man went out to shoot a deer, for hunger drove him to it . . . Which of us can feed this poor orphan lad?'

There was a general murmur of pity while the boy Much knelt weeping by his father's body. Then somebody said quietly:

'Robin Hood will not let him starve. Look, here comes his man, Will Scarlet, carrying a sack. May God and Our Lady bless this Robin Hood who comes to our aid like some very angel.'

A man had walked quickly into their midst as he spoke, a tall man of some forty years of age whose costume of russet and scarlet well suited the name by which these poor outcasts knew him.

'Have courage, my friends!' cried Will Scarlet, lowering the heavy sack as he spoke. 'My master and your true friend Robin Hood has sent me with this, fearing lest you should hunger. For he knows that the Sheriff and his men have been out in the Forest this day – and they ever leave misery and want behind them.'

'God's blessing on brave Robin Hood!' chorused all of them, except the boy who still knelt weeping by the still body.

Scarlet went over to him and laid a hand gently on his shoulder.

'So they have killed old Much,' he said. 'Have comfort, boy: he is at peace, and has been spared many evils. It was a quick death, see the arrow has transfixed his heart . . . Strange, that arrow never came from Nottingham armoury: it is such a one as my master and his servants use.'

'Good Will Scarlet!' cried the boy, turning to him

177

suddenly. 'Let me come with you and serve your noble master too. I know I am but twelve years old – but sorrow brings us quickly to manhood – and I would be revenged on these accursed murderers.'

'Speak not of revenge,' said Will Scarlet gently. 'It is for justice that we fight . . . But come with me. We have need of a bold lad like you – and one who can be trusted, even to the death as your father could be trusted.'

'Aye, aye,' chorused the group round about them. 'Be sure the old man died rather than betray your master, and so would any one of us. God save Robin Hood – King Richard and Robin Hood!'

2

HOW ROBERT OF LOCKSLEY BECAME AN OUTLAW

> This youth that leads you virgin by the hand
> Is our Earl Robert, or your Robin Hood
> That in these days was Earl of Huntingdon;
> The ill-fac'd miser, brib'd in either hand,
> Is Worman, once the steward of his house,
> Who, Judas like, betrays his liberal lord.
>
> ANTHONY MUNDAY: *The Downfall of Robert Earl of Huntingdon* (1601)

In Locksley Hall that night all seemed peaceful and happy enough as his friends and tenants feasted in honour of Robert Fitzooth's wedding with Marian Fitzwalter which was to take place on the morrow.

Earl Robert stood near the great fireplace welcoming his guests: a fine, well-built man of some thirty years, handsome, brown-haired with a short beard and clear eyes behind which seemed to lurk a shadow – of pity and of determination. All his movements were quick, but none of them was hurried; he was the man of action, the leader who could see things clearly and, in a flash, deliver his order and act upon his decision with swift accuracy and perfect coolness.

The Lady Marian Fitzwalter stood beside him. She was some five years younger than he, tall and beautiful, but strong and fearless also, a very fitting wife for such a man.

So certainly thought most of those present, as they came up in turns to offer their congratulations, or their services according to rank, or joined from time to time in a hearty song followed by the old Saxon pledge of 'Waes heal!' as they raised their goblets or silver-mounted horns of mead or ale to the two of them.

Two palmers however, who had come in late, led by Worman the steward, did not seem so eager in their toasts.

'I smell treason, there's no doubt of it!' muttered the darker of the two.

'It's a whole nest of traitors, your Highness,' agreed his companion. 'They'll give us proof before long, you may depend upon it!'

As if to bear out his words, a group of foresters dressed all in Lincoln green, who stood near the door, began to sing:

> Long live Richard,
>   Robin and Richard!
> Long live Richard!
>   Down with John!
> Drink to the Lion-heart
>   Everyone!

'Down with John, indeed!' said the dark palmer grimly. 'Now I trust that my disguise is good – and that master Worman, the false steward, won't waver again in his loyalties! Hallo, what have we here?'

As the song ended there was a slight stir near the doorway and a tall forester dressed in russet and scarlet appeared pushing his way through the throng, and leading a boy by the hand.

The second palmer stiffened suddenly like a pointer-dog smelling game.

'My lord,' he whispered to his companion. 'That boy is the son of old Much the Miller whom you saw shot this afternoon when he escaped from those who would so justly have burned out his eyes for deer-slaying on a second charge.'

'Indeed, my good Sheriff,' replied the supposed palmer. 'This false Earl Robert harbours the sons of traitors and criminals, does he? . . . But here comes Master Worman.'

'How now, Master Worman?' asked the disguised Sheriff in an undertone. 'What does this mean?'

'Yonder is Earl Robert's man, William Scathlock,' answered Worman, 'and he brings with him the son of that traitor who threatened your highness this afternoon, and in whose black heart I was lucky enough to plant an arrow.'

'Well?'

'Your Highness, when I inquired for Much the Miller's son – never mind from whom – they told me that all was well with him since a certain Will Scarlet had come and taken him away to be cared for by Robin Hood!'

'Will Scarlet! . . . Robin Hood,' mused Prince John, 'The devil! . . . Master Worman, and you, good Sir Sheriff, we are in better luck than ever we dreamed of! Do you not see? Will Scarlet takes Much to the care of Robin Hood . . . William Scathlock brings that same Much to the care of Robert Fitzooth – to that false Earl Robert who sells his lands and uses the proceeds so mysteriously . . . Why, my good fellows, it is proof positive . . . And that song they were singing:

Long live Richard,
Robin and Richard!

Yes, there's no doubt of it . . . Well, your fortunes are made. Tomorrow this traitor Robert or Robin is declared an outlaw – and you take and hang him forthwith. Then of course all his lands and goods are forfeit to me: I take them – and that attractive young heiress the Lady Marian lacks a husband . . . She has one waiting for her though, as I know well, and one true to my cause . . . Yes, Sir Guy of Gisborne shall have her – and with her father's good will, or I am much mistaken in my man . . . And Sir Guy shall pay me a fine fat dowry for his bride!'

No one suspected the two supposed palmers at Earl

Robert's feast, but none the less there was an air of anxiety over the wedding preparations in the chapel of Fountains Abbey next day.

Lord Fitzwalter seemed troubled and uneasy, though his daughter Marian was calm enough, even though she and her father stood waiting at the altar some time before Earl Robert rode up to the door with his troop of bowmen. Placing his men in the aisles in military formation – much to Lord Fitzwalter's surprise and the Abbot's indignation – Earl Robert only then came forward to take his place beside Marian.

Looking anything but pleased, the fat little Abbot began to intone the ceremony, his long lines of monks chanting the responses in the wide chancel behind him.

But before ever the words were spoken which would make Robert and Marian man and wife, there came the sound of galloping hooves, the clash and jingle of armour, and into the

chapel strode a knight with a drawn sword in his hand and followed by a band of men at arms.

'What means this sacrilege?' cried the Abbot, torn between fear and indignation.

'Hold!' cried the knight. 'I, Sir Guy of Gisborne, come in the King's name to forbid this ceremony to proceed! Pursuivant, read the mandate!'

A man dressed in the livery of the Sheriff of Nottingham stepped forward, unrolled a parchment, and read in a loud voice:

'Be it known to all, in the name of Prince John, Regent of all England, that Robert Fitzooth, known as Robert Earl of Huntingdon – known also as Robin Hood; for as much as he hath aided the King's enemies, broken the King's laws, and is a traitor to the King and to those by him set in authority; that the same Robert Fitzooth or Robin Hood is hereby declared outlaw, his lands and goods forfeit, and his person proscribed and banished. In the name of Richard our King and of the Regent, Prince John!'

'Sir Guy,' said Robert quietly, 'this is an ill quest you come on, and all unworthy of the high order of knighthood which you profess. As for this mandate, I question its force! Show me King Richard's seal attached to it . . . You cannot. Show me then the Seal of My Lord Bishop of Ely the King's only lawfully appointed Regent . . . Why, that is missing from the mandate also! . . . Tell me wherein I have played the part of a traitor – and, wherefore I, Robert Fitzooth, Esquire of Locksley and Earl of Huntingdon, should answer for the supposed misdeeds of this mythical wood-demon called Robin Hood who is surely no more than a bogey raised by the credulity and superstition of the ignorant!'

Guy of Gisborne laughed harshly.

'This is no time for jests and fairy tales,' he cried. 'We all know that you have ever flouted the laws and striven to set the serfs against their masters. Why, the very act of calling yourself Earl of Huntingdon in right of your mother's Saxon forbears shows you as a traitor: the old Saxon earls were deprived and outlawed for refusing to obey their rightful King, William of Normandy, and only the Earldom created by the King has any right in law. As for your trespasses in the matter of the Forest Laws – everyone knows your skill in archery – and there are few travellers in these parts who have not eaten the King's venison under your roof. Finally, it is useless to pretend ignorance of the crimes committed by you under the false name of Robin Hood. How many among your own followers are proscribed felons who are said to belong to Robin Hood's band? . . . What of his lieutenant who is also of your household? . . . What of Much, the Miller's son, whom Robin Hood has under his care – in your house of Locksley Hall?'

'Why, then,' came the quiet answer, 'here and now Robert Fitzooth, Earl of Huntingdon, ceases to be. You have called me Robin Hood: both you and your Sheriff – yes and Prince John himself shall live to fear that name. And not only you, but all those like you: the abbots and bishops who grow fat on the sufferings of the poor; the Norman knights and barons who break both the King's law and the law of God in their cruelties and oppressions – yes, and all their kind shall go in terror so long as Robin Hood reigns in Sherwood Forest: in Sherwood, and wherever else wrongs need to be righted – until King Richard comes home from the Crusade and there is justice once more in this fair land of England.'

Then, turning to Marian Fitzwalter who had stood all this while by his side, Robin said gently:

'Lady Marian, did you give your love to the Earl of Huntingdon whose lands stretch from the Trent to the Ouse, or to plain Robin Hood the outlaw who returns now to the home of his birth under the green leaves of Sherwood Forest?'

'Neither to the Earl nor to his Earldom,' answered Marian firmly, 'but to the man whom I love and whose wife alone I shall be.'

'Indeed, I thought no other,' said Robin gravely, 'and though the ceremony is but half completed, I hold that we are none the less man and wife in the sight of God and of this congregation . . . Lord Fitzwalter, to your care I commit your daughter: guard her well at Arlingford Castle, and I will demand her of you again when King Richard is here to place her hand in mine.'

'To that also I swear!' cried Marian. 'You, Robin, are my

lord and my husband, and no other shall ever be aught to me, though I live and die a maid!'

'Go quickly now,' said Robin to Lord Fitzwalter, 'and go you quickly with him, sweet Marian. No, you cannot help me: when I have beaten off these curs, I ride to the merry greenwood, there to set up my court!'

'Come now, false traitor and outlaw Robin Hood!' cried Guy of Gisborne. 'Out of your own mouth are you convicted of treason many times over before this company – whom I call upon to witness . . . Come now, deliver up your sword and submit yourself to the authority of your undoubted lord, Prince John. If you do so, there may still be mercy for you!'

'He knows of no mercy!' cried Robin. 'Prince John knows only the desires of his own evil heart – and you do ill to serve him . . . As for my sword, I deliver it up to John and his officers – thus!'

With a sudden lightning movement Robin whipped the sword from his side and smote Guy of Gisborne such a blow upon his iron helmet that he stumbled and fell to the ground insensible. Then he charged down the nave, his men closing in from either side as he went, and a short sharp battle took place near the chapel door.

'Help! Murder! Sacrilege!' shouted the fat Abbot, and his monks and friars took up the cry as they pushed and crowded in their eagerness to escape through the narrow door which led to the Abbey. They were speeded on their way by an occasional arrow from Robin's archers who continued to send shaft after shaft among Sir Guy's followers until they too fell back towards the door by which the Abbot had already squeezed his way into safety.

When the sound of horses' hooves told him that Lord Fitzwalter with Marian and their followers were well away in the direction of Arlingford Castle, Robin gave the signal to his men, and with one determined charge they were out of the chapel and away through Sherwood Forest in the direction of Locksley Hall.

Sir Guy, still half stunned, was only just raising himself from the floor of the chapel, and Robin had disappeared with all his following into the green depths of Sherwood by the time he had gathered his wits and staggered to his feet.

'There's no use in following him now, God's malaison upon this rogue Fitzooth and his friends!' he exclaimed. 'But he'll find the Sheriff and Master Worman waiting for him at Locksley Hall if he ventures there!'

Bidding those of his followers who still stood upon their feet attend to those whom Robin's followers had laid out on the chapel floor, Sir Guy made his way into the Abbey, where the Abbot was only too ready to entertain him to dinner.

'An unholy scoundrel!' spluttered the Abbot, who needed his goblet filling again and yet again with choice wine before he could recover from the shock to his dignity and the terror of those terrible whizzing arrows. 'He is well outlawed. May a blessing rest upon the head of the man who cuts him off!'

'A dangerous fellow,' agreed Sir Guy, putting his hand to his aching head. 'And I grieve that he escaped us for now he will grow more dangerous.'

'Earl Robert is a worthy man,' remarked a friar who was quite the tallest, broadest, and reddest in the face of any there. 'He is the best marksman in England and can outshoot any forester or archer both for distance and for directness of aim.'

'Brother Michael! Brother Michael!' puffed the Abbot. 'You speak treason! How can an outlaw be a worthy man? And as for his skill as an archer –'

'He will draw the long bow with any yeoman,' interrupted Brother Michael placidly, 'and split a willow wand at two hundred paces!'

'Be that as it may,' said Sir Guy, glowering at the friar, 'he is an outlaw now – and the sooner an arrow reaches his heart the better.'

'It is a dangerous thing to outlaw such a man,' boomed Brother Michael. 'You have taken his home: where will he live? Why, in the Forest! You have taken his cattle and his swine: what will he eat? Why, the King's deer! You have robbed him of money and goods – why then, he will rob you and all of your kind. Oh-ho, no knight nor sheriff, no abbot nor bishop will be safe from him now!'

'All the more reason why we should catch him swiftly and string him to a gallows!' snapped Sir Guy. 'But father Abbot, tell me of the Lady Marian: how came Lord Fitzwalter to betroth her to such a man as Fitzooth – for surely neither father nor daughter can have been ignorant that he was Robin Hood?'

'Oh, she is a fine lass, truly!' cried Brother Michael before the Abbot could get in a word. 'I am her confessor, and indeed I should know! Has she not beauty, grace, wit, good sense and high valour? Can she not fence with the sword, ply the quarter-staff and shoot with the long bow all but as well as – as Robin Hood himself? Truly a worthy mate for a worthy man: I would, sir knight, that you had delayed your coming but a brief half-hour, and a knot would have been tied that all our usurper Prince John's mandates could not have untied.'

'My sword would have cut it soon enough!' shouted Sir Guy. 'And it is only your cloth, master friar, that saves your head from feeling the edge of that same sword.'

'Oh, the penances I will impose upon you for this!' began the Abbot, turning to Brother Michael and almost bursting with rage.

'Why then, holy father,' cried the friar, 'I will not be here to suffer them! I have a ready welcome at Arlingford Castle – and thither I will hasten and take up my abode.'

'And I will accompany you,' said Guy of Gisborne grimly. 'This paragon of beauty, the Lady Marian, is well worth a visit – and may well prove a bait that will draw this outlawed Robin Hood into a trap.'

3

THE OUTLAWS OF SHERWOOD FOREST

An hundred valiant men had this brave Robin Hood,
Still ready at his call, that bowmen were right good,
All clad in Lincoln green, with caps of red and blue,
His fellow's winded horn not one of them but knew . . .
All made of Spanish yew, their bows were wondrous
                    strong;
They not an arrow drew but was a clothyard long.

MICHAEL DRAYTON: *Polyolbion xxvi* (1622)

Early next morning Sir Guy of Gisborne set out for Arlingford Castle, his guide being the fat Friar called Brother Michael who had so disgraced himself on the previous night by praising the outlawed Robin Hood.

The Friar rode at his side singing lustily – in spite of the fact that as they left the Abbey, the Abbot had banished him in no uncertain terms: 'You go out, false and traitorous man, as you came in many years ago – plain Michael Tuck – no longer a Brother of this Order. If you show your face at my doors again, my doors will be shut in your face!'

'Why then!' cried the Friar gaily, 'farewell to the Abbey of Fountains, and all hail to the jolly greenwood – and catch me again if you can!'

So he went on his way, singing:

> For hark! hark! hark!
> The dog doth bark,
>   That watches the wild deer's lair,
> The hunter awakes at the peep of the dawn,
> But the lair it is empty, the deer it is gone,
>   And the hunter knows not where!

As they came in sight of Arlingford Castle the Friar ceased from his singing, and turning to Sir Guy, remarked:

'You had best turn back, sir knight – or at the least lower that vizor of yours!'

'How?' exclaimed Guy of Gisborne. 'Surely Lord Fitzwalter is not in league with Robin Hood?'

'Far from it!' laughed the fat Friar, 'but Lady Marian Fitwalter assuredly is. And Lady Marian is as apt with an arrow as most damsels are with a needle!'

They reached the castle in safety, however, and Lord Fitzwalter welcomed them loudly, showing great eagerness to be on the side in power:

'You have done me a wrong? How so? Would you have had me marry my daughter to an outlaw, a fly-by-night, a slayer of the King's deer – and of the Prince's followers? A man who flings away an earldom, broad lands and rich treasures to help a lot of miserable serfs and other riff-raff most justly persecuted by the laws of the land. No, sir, no:

you have done me a service. A great service. I have finished with Fitzooth, or Robin Hood, or whatever that rascally beggar now calls himself. And so has my daughter.'

'And yet she is half wedded to him by the dictates of the Church,' remarked the Friar, 'and wholly his by the dictates of her heart.'

'The marriage was not completed!' shouted Lord Fitzwalter. 'Therefore I care nothing for it. As for love – it is your business, as her confessor, to show her that her love for this traitor is sinful and to be stamped out!'

'Marriages,' quoth the Friar, 'are made in Heaven. Love is God's work – and it is not for me to meddle with it.'

'The ceremony was cut short – sure proof that Heaven laid no blessing on it!' roared Lord Fitzwalter. 'Besides, I betrothed my daughter to the Earl of Huntingdon, not to the outlawed traitor Robin Hood.'

'He may be pardoned,' answered the Friar. 'Coeur de Lion is a worthy King – and Fitzooth a worthy peer.'

'There can be no pardon,' said Sir Guy hastily. 'He has killed the King's subjects and defied the King's sheriff.'

Lord Fitzwalter was growing more and more red in the face with fury, but at this moment the Lady Marian came suddenly into the room, clad in Lincoln green, with a quiver of arrows at her side and a bow in her hand.

'How now?' roared her father. 'Where are you off to now, wench?'

'To the greenwood,' said Marian calmly.

'That you shall not!' bellowed Lord Fitzwalter.

'But I am going,' said Marian.

'But I will have up the drawbridge.'

'But I will swim the moat.'

'But I will secure the gates.'

'But I will leap from the battlement.'

'But I will lock you in an upper chamber.'

'But I will shred the tapestry and let myself down.'

'But I will lock you in a turret where you shall only see light through a loophole.'

'But I will find some way of escape. And, father, while I go freely, I shall return willingly. But once shut me up, and if I slip out then, I shall not return at all . . . Robin waits for me in the greenwood, and the knot half-tied yesterday can so easily be tied completely.'

'Well spoken, lady,' cried the Friar.

'Ill spoken, Friar!' thundered Lord Fitzwalter. 'Get out of my castle this instant! You are in league with the traitor Robin Hood, I know it! If you come here again, I'll have you whipped, monk or no monk!'

'I go, I go!' said the Friar calmly. 'I know of a hermitage by the riverside where I may well take up my abode – and levy toll on all those who would pass by: payment, of course, for my prayers! Abbey and castle have cast me out, but not so easily shall Friar Tuck be cast down!'

And away he strode, singing blithely:

> For I must seek some hermit cell,
> Where I alone my beads may tell,
> And on the wight who that way fares,
> Levy a toll for my ghostly pray'rs!

'So much for an impudent friar,' puffed Lord Fitzwalter. 'Now for a wayward girl!'

'A husband,' said Sir Guy with meaning, 'is the best curb for such as she.'

'Aye, a husband – and of my choosing!' agreed Lord Fitzwalter. 'No more earls of doubtful earldoms, but, shall we say, a knight with definite lands and treasures, and definitely in favour with Prince John! Such a man, in fact, as – well, no matter!'

Lord Fitzwalter looked Guy of Gisborne up and down with approval, but Marian broke out:

'No man of your choosing, father – unless he be my choice also. And my choice is and will ever be for brave Robin Hood!'

'I'll keep you in a dungeon and feed you on bread and water!' thundered Lord Fitzwalter.

'Robin will sack your castle to rescue me,' said Marian gaily. Then suddenly serious, she exclaimed: 'Father, you will let me go to the greenwood? You have my promise that I will return. And I promise also that Robin shall be nothing more to me than he is now, without your leave – or until King Richard return and give me to him in marriage with his own hand.'

189

Then, blowing a kiss to her father, and paying no attention whatsoever to Guy of Gisborne, Marian tripped gaily from the room and away into Sherwood Forest.

'And now,' said Lord Fitzwalter grimly, 'it is for you to catch this outlaw and string him up to the highest gallows in Nottinghamshire. Until that is done, I fear there will be no use in your coming here to ask my daughter's hand in marriage.'

Sir Guy rose and bowed to his host.

'My lord,' he said, 'I am already on my way to Locksley Hall. The Sheriff's men were to surround it last night, taking prisoner any who came in or out, and my followers do but await me at the Abbey. When I get there, it may well be to find Robin Hood already in their hands.'

But Robert Fitzooth had not been so unaware of the dangers into which his double life as Robin Hood was leading him as the Sheriff and Prince John had supposed. When he escaped from the chapel after the interrupted wedding, Robin and some twenty men at arms rode off into Sherwood Forest and continued on their way to within a mile or so of Locksley Hall. Here Robin halted and turning, spoke to his followers:

'My friends, what I feared has befallen me. You all heard the mandate of outlawry read against me – and some of you may have incurred danger of the same by withstanding those men sent against me under Sir Guy of Gisborne. Well now, you may choose for yourselves: I set you all free from my service – but indeed as I am an outlaw, that sets you free whether I will or no. If you did not all know it already, you know now that I am that Robin Hood who, for several years now, has befriended all such as suffer under the cruelty and unjustness of lords, barons, bishops, abbots and sheriffs. I have already a band of men sworn to follow me who await me in the greenwood: we are all comrades and brothers, though me they have chosen to be their leader and their king – not because I am by right an Earl, not merely because I have the gift of a steady hand and a clear eye and so can shoot an arrow further and straighter than most men, but because one must rule and I come of a race of rulers (though we are but slaves now to our Norman masters). I am no more Robert

Fitzooth, Earl of Huntingdon, but the plain yeoman of Locksley whom men call Robin Hood: but my friends in Sherwood have chosen me king, and a king in Sherwood I shall be, my first care for my followers, but our first care for justice and mercy and the love of God. And in this I hold that we commit no treason: when Richard comes home from the Crusade this reign of terror and of evil against which I fight will end. Cruel, lawless John will oppress us no longer, nor his friends and followers use us without right or justice, as slaves and not as free men.

'Choose now, will you follow me into Sherwood, all such of you as have neither wife nor child – or, as you blamelessly may, go back to serve the new master of Locksley. Only, for the love and service that was between us, I charge you to betray neither me nor any who were your companions and are now mine.'

Then most of the men at arms cried aloud that they would follow Robin Hood through weal and woe, and all swore that they would die rather than betray him. Some then turned and with bent heads rode off towards Locksley – drawn thither by wife or child – and swore reluctantly to serve Sir Guy of Gisborne so long as he might be the master of Locksley.

'And now,' said Robin to those who remained with him, 'let us away to our new home in the forest and see how many of us there be who stand loyally together for God, for His anointed servant Richard, King by right divine, and for justice and the righting of wrongs.'

Deep in the heart of Sherwood Forest, as the sun was setting behind them, Robin and his men came to a great glade where stood the greatest of all the forest oaks upon a stretch of open greensward with steep banks fencing it on either hand in which were caves both deep and dry. At either end of the shallow valley, and beyond the banks on each side, the forest hedged them in with its mighty trees, with oak and ash, with beech and elm and chestnut, and also with thick clumps of impassable thorns, with desolate marshes where an unwary step might catch a man or a horse and drag him down into the dark quagmire, and with brambles rising like high dikes and knolls through which even a man in armour could scarcely force his way.

For the last mile Robin led by narrow, winding paths, pointing out to his companions the secret, hidden signs by which they could find their way.

Once in the glade, Robin took the horn from his belt and blew on it a blast which echoed away and away into the distance. Already men dressed smartly in doublet and hose of Lincoln green, in hoods of green or russet and in knee-boots of soft brown leather, had come out from the caves to greet them.

At a few brief words, they set about lighting two great fires near the oak tree in the glade, and roasting great joints of venison before them. They also brought coarse loaves of brown bread, and rolled out two barrels of ale, setting up rough trestle tables with logs in lieu of stools.

As the darkness grew, men kept appearing silently in the glade and taking their place by the fires or at the tables until a company of fifty or sixty was gathered together.

Then Robin Hood rose up and addressed them. He began by telling them, as he had told the men at arms, of his banishment, and reminding them that they were outlaws, but not robbers.

'We must take the King's deer,' he ended, 'since we must eat to live. But when the King returns I myself will beg pardon at his feet for this trespass. And now you shall all swear the oath which I swear with you, and all seeking to join us must swear also. We declare war upon all of those thieves, robbers, extortioners and men of evil whom we find among the nobles, the clergy, and burgesses of town – in particular those who follow or accompany Prince John; false abbots, monks, bishops and archbishops, whom we will beat and bind like sheaves of corn so that they may yield the golden grain of their robberies – the Abbots of St Mary's, Doncaster, and Fountains shall we seek for in particular; and I think we shall keep within our oath if we make it our especial care to harry and persecute the false Sheriff of Nottingham who so wickedly abuses his power to please and satisfy his master Prince John.

'Now, my friends, we do not take from these and their kind to enrich ourselves. We take for the general good, and it shall be as much our duty to seek out the poor, the needy, the widow, the orphan and all those who have suffered or are suffering wrong, and minister to their wants in so far as we can.

'We shall swear, moreover, to harm no woman, be she Norman or Saxon, high or low, but to succour and assist any who crave our aid or need our protection, dealing with them with all honesty and purity, seeing in every woman the likeness of Our Lady the Holy Mary, Mother of Christ, in whose name we take our oath, and by whose name we dedicate ourselves to the service of the true Church, and to whom we pray to intercede for us before the throne of God that we may have strength to keep this our oath in the face of all temptations.'

Then, in that wild and lonely glade, while the owls screamed over the dark forest, and an occasional wolf howled in the distance, they all knelt down together and swore their oath – a pledge as high and as sacred, though they were but outlaws and escaped felons, as that sworn by the noblest knight who, in the days when the Saxons themselves were the conquerors and oppressors, had sat at King Arthur's Table.

(from The Adventures of Robin Hood, 1956)

Babes in the Wood

O, don't you remember a long time ago
Those two little babies their names I don't know,
They strayed away one bright summer's day,
Those two little babies got lost on their way.
Pretty babes in the wood, pretty babes in the wood,
O, don't you remember those babes in the wood?

Now the day being done and the night coming on
Those two little babies sat under a stone.
They sobbed and they sighed they sat there and cried,
Those two little babies they lay down and died.
Pretty babes in the wood, pretty babes in the wood,
O, don't you remember those babes in the wood?

Now the robins so red how swiftly they sped,
They put out their wide wings and over them spread.
And all the day long in the branches they throng,
They sweetly did whistle and this was their song,
Pretty babes in the wood, pretty babes in the wood,
O, don't you remember those babes in the wood?

JIM COPPER

O don't you re-mem-ber a long time a-go Those
two lit-tle bab-ies their names I don't know They
strayed a-way one bright sum-mer's day Those
two lit-tle bab-ies got lost on their way Pret-ty
babes in the wood pret-ty babes in the wood O
don't you re-mem-ber those babes in the wood.

The Passionate Shepherd to His Love

Come live with me and be my Love,
And we will all the pleasures prove
That hills and valleys, dale and field,
And all the craggy mountains yield.

There will we sit upon the rocks
And see the shepherds feed their flocks,
By shallow rivers, to whose falls
Melodious birds sing madrigals.

There will I make thee beds of roses
And a thousand fragrant posies,
A cap of flowers, and a kirtle
Embroidered all with leaves of myrtle.

A gown made of the finest wool,
Which from our pretty lambs we pull,
Fair lined slippers for the cold,
With buckles of the purest gold.

A belt of straw and ivy buds
With coral clasps and amber studs;
And if these pleasures may thee move,
Come live with me and be my love.

Thy silver dishes for thy meat
As precious as the gods do eat,
Shall on an ivory table be
Prepared each day for thee and me.

The shepherd swains shall dance and sing
For thy delight each May-morning:
If these delights thy mind may move,
Then live with me and be my love.

CHRISTOPHER MARLOWE

The Nymph's Reply

If all the world and love were young,
And truth in every shepherd's tongue,
These pretty pleasures might me move
To live with thee and be thy Love.

But Time drives flocks from field to fold;
When rivers rage and rocks grow cold;
And Philomel becometh dumb;
The rest complains of cares to come.

The flowers do fade, and wanton fields
To wayward Winter reckoning yields:
A honey tongue, a heart of gall,
Is fancy's spring, but sorrow's fall.

Thy gowns, thy shoes, thy beds of roses,
Thy cap, thy kirtle, and thy posies,
Soon break, soon wither – soon forgotten,
In folly ripe, in reason rotten.

Thy belt of straw and ivy-buds,
Thy coral clasps and amber studs –
All these in me no means can move
To come to thee and be thy Love.

But could youth last, and love still breed,
Had joys no date, nor age no need,
Then these delights my mind might move
To live with thee and be thy Love.

SIR WALTER RALEGH

The Poacher

RICHARD WILLIAMSON

By the tree, sheltered by the warmth of the trunk, the poacher had stood listening to sounds for an hour. He had heard the movement of rabbits going out of the wood to feed. A mouse had run over his boot. Owls had called, from far off or near, and they had gone hunting, wailing to one another. He was listening for the low murmur of an engine, or the mumble of boots over the hard ground, or a pheasant alarmed. Once, wild duck had passed overhead, close to the stars. He felt a warmth of excitement at winter's coming, and the sport. A woodcock went by; he could see the wings which seemed not to be moving. Then he forgot about the grey man, and when a pheasant rang *cuck-uck-cuck-uck-cuck* in the hardening air it was not because the slow wandering of the grey man had frightened it but a distant rumble of thunder, or guns, or an explosion, which he could not hear himself. He thought to light a fag, but kept still, knowing how the air could carry the smell half a mile. Then, when he was ready to move, seeing the moon rising in fragments through the trees, he heard a sound of dead leaves trampled. He got close in to the tree, thinking it to be the grey man. But when it came closer he could hear four feet moving in the leaves. The sound wandered about. He heard a twig being pulled and knew it was a deer. The animal did not seem as though it could see him. It came close but must have been hidden behind a thicket. He thought of the small shot in the cartridge, and decided to risk a neck shot at close range. Very slowly he moved over to one side to get the deer in view. Then he knew he had been seen. The deer had jumped and then stood still. The slowly creeping moon, like a grub in the sky, showed nothing, except the greater darkness of trees. After a while he felt sure he could see the deer moving about; it moved to the left, it came closer, it moved back. But there was silence. He tried looking far to one side, to see it from

the corner of the eye, a trick of poachers. But it was no use.
He thought of the deer watching him, able to stand for hours
waiting for the first move, and he thought of its hot blood
on his fingers and the pounds of meat, perhaps a week's
wages or a month's meat for his family. He thought to try a
shot at a dark place in front. At that moment the deer moved.
It was not the relaxed feeding walk. It was the slow walk of
the watcher. He heard it in the leaves moving away, then to
his left. Very gently he twisted on his heels and followed its
movements. It was circling him. He knew it was after his
scent, but he wasn't sure where that would lie. As he turned
the trees seemed to revolve against the stars. After a while
he was facing the moon, and in that second the deer stopped,
with its head breaking the outline of the moon. The deer was
quite close. The hairs surrounding its two ears were feathered
with a light halo. He could see little else of it. It was such a
quiet moment. His heart was banging, but the deer seemed
unafraid, almost as if it were a dog standing there next to
him. He began to raise the gun. The deer barked. The
poacher pulled the trigger before the gun was to his shoulder.

He saw a column of orange sparks, but nothing else. He ran forward, stabbing his eyeball on a twig, but hardly noticing this; he felt excitedly among the dead leaves for the body. It had only been a few yards off. Then he thought to stop and listen, in case the deer was wounded and was dragging in the leaves. There was silence. Again he searched, on hands and knees, feeling between the bushes and coppice until his hands were black with mould. He had dropped the gun somewhere behind. There was nothing there to find. He stopped and listened again. An owl wailed far away in the woods . . .

(from *Capreol: The Story of a Roebuck*, 1974)

*

The Mole-Catcher

Tattered and ragg'd, with greatcoat tied in strings,
And collared up to keep his chin from cold,
The old mole-catcher on his journey sings,
Followed by shaggy dog infirm and old,
Who potters on and keeps his steady pace;
He is so lame he scarce can get abroad
But hopples on and growls at anything;
Yet silly sheep will scarcely leave the road.
With stick and spud he tries the new-made hills
And bears his cheating traps from place to place;
Full many are the miners that he kills.
His trotting dog oft looks him in the face;
And when his toils are done he tries to play
And finds a quicker pace and barks him on his way.

JOHN CLARE

Forest Brotherhood

It was a clear and sunny day, the weather had been still and dry for a whole week.

The usual rumble of noise hung over the large camp, rather like the distant roar of the sea. There were footsteps, voices, axes chopping wood, the ringing of an anvil, the barking of dogs, the neighing of horses and the crowing of cocks. Crowds of sunburnt, white-toothed, smiling men moved about the forest. Those who knew the doctor nodded to him, others passed him by without a greeting.

The men had refused to strike camp until their families, who were fleeing from their homes, had caught up with them, but now the fugitives were expected shortly and preparations for the move were being made. Things were being cleaned and mended, crates nailed down and carts counted and checked over.

There was a large clearing in the middle of the wood where meetings were often held; it was a sort of mound or barrow on which the grass had been trodden down. A general meeting had been called that day for some important announcement.

Many of the trees in the forest had not yet turned yellow. In its depths they were still fresh and green. The afternoon sun, sinking behind the forest, pierced it with its rays, and the leaves, transparent as glass, shone with a green flame.

On an open space outside his tent Kamennodversky, the chief liaison officer, was burning papers, discarding rubbish from General Kappel's records which had fallen into his hands, as well as his own partisan files. The fire, with the setting sun behind it, was as transparent as the leaves; the flames were invisible and only the waves of shimmering heat showed that something was burning.

Here and there the woods were brilliant with ripe berries – bright tassels of lady's-smock, brick-red alderberries and clusters of viburnum which changed from white to purple. Tinkling their glassy wings, dragon-flies, as transparent as the flames and the leaves, sailed slowly through the air.

Ever since his childhood Yury had been fond of woods seen at evening against the setting sun. At such moments he felt as if he too were being pierced by blades of light. As if the gift of the living spirit were streaming into his breast, piercing his being and coming out by his shoulders like a pair of wings. The archetype, which is formed in every child for life and seems for ever after to be the inward image of his personality, arose in him in its full primordial strength and compelled nature, the forest, the afterglow and everything else visible to be transfigured into a similarly primordial and all-embracing likeness of a girl. 'Lara.' Closing his eyes, he whispered and thought, addressing the whole of life, all God's earth, all the sunlit space spread out before him.

But the everyday, current reality was still there: Russia was going through the October Revolution and Yury was a prisoner of the partisans.

(from *Doctor Zhivago*, 1957)

*

A Lover and His Lass

It was a lover and his lass,
    With a hey, and a ho, and a hey nonino,
That o'er the green cornfield did pass
    In springtime, the only pretty ring time,
When birds do sing, hey ding a ding, ding;
Sweet lovers love the spring.

Between the acres of the rye,
    With a hey, and a ho, and a hey nonino,
These pretty country folks would lie
    In springtime, the only pretty ring time,
When birds do sing, hey ding a ding, ding;
Sweet lovers love the spring.

This carol they began that hour,
    With a hey, and a ho, and a hey nonino,
How that life was but a flower
    In springtime, the only pretty ring time,
When birds do sing, hey ding a ding, ding;
Sweet lovers love the spring.

And therefore take the present time,
    With a hey, and a ho, and a hey nonino,
For love is crowned with the prime
    In springtime, the only pretty ring time,
When birds do sing, hey ding a ding, ding;
Sweet lovers love the spring.

(from *As You Like It*)   WILLIAM SHAKESPEARE

A Shropshire Lad

Along the field as we came by
A year ago, my love and I,
The aspen over stile and stone
Was talking to itself alone.
'Oh who are these that kiss and pass?
A country lover and his lass;
Two lovers looking to be wed;
And time shall put them both to bed,
But she shall lie with earth above,
And he beside another love.'

And sure enough beneath the tree
There walks another love with me,
And overhead the aspen heaves
Its rainy-sounding silver leaves;
And I spell nothing in their stir,
But now perhaps they speak to her,
And plain for her to understand
They talk about a time at hand
When I shall sleep with clover clad,
And she beside another lad.

A. E. HOUSMAN

The Forest People

COLIN TURNBULL

In his fascinating book The Forest People, *Colin Turnbull tells of the lives of the pygmies who live in nomadic camps in the Ituri Forest. This is a 'vast expanse of dense, damp and inhospitable-looking darkness' in the middle of Africa, in the north-east corner of the country now called Zaïre. Colin Turnbull lived among these people for three years; he speaks their language and was accepted as their friend.*

I have chosen three short passages from the book. The last passage describes the author's feelings on walking through the forest when he had only two months left among the pygmies. He is with one of them, Kenge; they have just returned from a trip into parts of the forest far away from the pygmies' home.

*

Anyone who has stood in the silent emptiness of a tropical rain forest must know how Stanley and his followers felt, coming as they all did from an open country of rolling plains, of sunlight and warmth. Many people who have visited the Ituri since, and many who have lived there, feel just the same – overpowered by the heaviness of everything; the damp air, the gigantic, water-laden trees that are constantly dripping, never quite drying out between the violent storms that come with monotonous regularity, the very earth itself becoming heavy and cloying after the slightest shower. And above all such people feel overpowered by the seeming silence and the age-old remoteness and loneliness of it all.

But these are the feelings of outsiders, of those who do not belong to the forest. If you *are* of the forest it is a very different place. What seems to other people to be eternal and depressing gloom becomes a cool, restful, shady world with light filtering lazily through the tree-tops that meet high overhead and shut out the forest sunlight – sunlight that dries up the non-forest world of the outsiders and makes it hot and dusty and dirty. Even the silence felt by others is a myth. If you have ears for it the forest is full of different sounds; exciting, mysterious, mournful, joyful. The shrill trumpeting of an elephant or the sickening cough of a leopard (or the hundred and one sounds that can be mistaken for it), always make your heart beat a little unevenly, telling you that you are just the slightest bit scared, or even more. At night, in the honey season, you hear a weird, long, drawn-out, soulful cry high up in the trees. It seems to go on and on, and you wonder what kind of creature can cry for so long without taking breath. The people of the forest say it is the chameleon, telling them that there is honey nearby. Scientists will tell you that chameleons are unable to make any such sound. But in far away Ceylon the forest people there also know the song of the chameleon.

Then in the early morning comes the pathetic cry of the pigeon, a plaintive cooing that slides from one note down to the next until it dies away in a soft, sad little moan.

There are a multitude of sounds, but most of them are as joyful as the brightly coloured birds that chase each other through the trees, singing as they go; or the chatter of the handsome black-and-white Colobus monkeys as they leap from branch to branch, watching with curiosity everything that goes on down below. And the most joyful sound of all, to me, is the sound of the voices of the forest people as they sing a lusty chorus of praise to this wonderful world of theirs – a world that gives them everything they want – a cascade of sound that echoes among the giant trees until it seems to come at you from all sides in sheer beauty and truth and goodness, full of the joy of living. And so it is, unless you are an outsider from the non-forest world, the world of human animals and savages, then I suppose this glorious song of real human beings would just be another noise to grate on your nerves . . .

In the very dead of night I could hear the sound of crickets from the forest, reminding me that it was, after all, not so far away, and all around us. Sometimes when the moon was full I wandered around the sleeping village, to the edges of the

plantations. There the forest stood up into the night like a great black wall, encircling this small circle, cut so ineffectively out of its very heart. It rose up all around, confident in the knowledge that it would soon claim its own and grow back more thickly than ever, where it had been cut. There were several such overgrown villages near by not long abandoned; yet already the forest towered above. The forest destroyed everything but its own. Only against the machine age, which had barely reached it, was it powerless.

In the very early hours the forest made itself felt, but close as it was it faded far away with the coming of dawn. The morning sounds of cocks crowing, goats bleating, and the elephants of the *Station de Chasse* as they were put through their exercises, all obscured the faint chirpings of crickets and birds and the chatter of monkeys. And as the sun rose and began to beat down on the parched and scorched earth, the village asserted once more its determination to dominate the hostile world around it . . .

It was, I knew, to be my last trek into the forest with the people I had come to think of as such close friends, and even though I knew I still had another two months with them I was sad. It was partly because of this, and partly because, like Kenge, I was so profoundly content to be back in our own part of the forest; and partly because Kenge also knew that this would be our last journey together, that I found the forest more beautiful than it had ever been. Kenge said it was just because it was the honey season, but as we passed the plantation and entered once more into the shade of the great, friendly old trees, he added: 'This is the *real* world . . . this is a good world, our forest.' He, too, was glad to be home.

(from *The Forest People*, 1961)

*

The Pigs and the Charcoal-Burner

The old Pig said to the little pigs,
  'In the forest is truffles and mast,
Follow me, then, all ye little pigs,
  Follow me fast!'

The Charcoal-burner sat in the shade
  With his chin on his thumb,
And saw the big Pig and the little pigs
  Chuffling come.

He watched 'neath a green and giant bough,
  And the pigs in the ground
Made a wonderful grizzling and gruzzling
  And greedy sound.

And when, full-fed, they were gone, and Night
  Walked her starry ways,
He stared with his cheek in his hands
  At his sullen blaze.

WALTER DE LA MARE

The Scarecrow

All winter through I bow my head
   Beneath the driving rain;
The North Wind powders me with snow
   Then blows me black again;
At midnight in a maze of stars
   I flame with glittering rime,
And stand, above the stubble, stiff
   As mail at morning-time.
But when that child, called Spring, and all
   His host of children, come,
Scattering their buds and dew upon
   These acres of my home,
Some rapture in my rags awakes;
   I lift void eyes and scan
The sky for crows, those ravening foes,
   Of my strange master, Man.
I watch him striding lank behind
   His clashing team and know
Soon will the wheat swish body high
   Where once lay sterile snow;
Soon shall I gaze across a sea
   Of sun-begotten grain,
Which my unflinching watch hath sealed
   For harvest once again.

WALTER DE LA MARE

Suffolk Ploughmen

RONALD BLYTHE

This Suffolk villager was eighty-eight when he talked to Ronald Blythe about his life as a farmer. As a boy he had worked for a landowner 'famous for his horses'.

*

The horses were friends and loved like men. Some men would do more for a horse than they would for a wife. The ploughmen talked softly to their teams all day long and you could see the horses listening. Although the teams ploughed twenty yards apart, the men didn't talk much to each other, except sometimes they sang. Each man ploughed in his own fashion and with his own mark. It looked all the same if you didn't know about ploughing, but a farmer could walk on a field ploughed by ten different teams and tell which bit was ploughed by which. Sometimes he would pay a penny an acre extra for perfect ploughing. Or he would make a deal with the ploughman – 'free rent for good work'. That could mean £5 a year. The men worked perfectly to get this, but they also worked perfectly because it was *their* work. It belonged to them. It was theirs.

The plough-teams left at seven sharp in the morning and finished at three in the afternoon. They reckoned a ploughman would walk eleven miles a day on average. It wasn't hard walking in the dirt, not like the rough roads. The horsemen were the big men on the farm. They kept in with each other and had secrets. They were a whispering lot. If someone who wasn't a ploughman came upon them and they happened to be talking, they'd soon change the conversation! And if you disturbed them in a room where the horse medicine was, it was covered up double quick. They made the horses obey with a sniff from a rag which they kept in their pockets. Caraway seeds had something to do with it, I believe, although others say different.

A lot of farmers hid their horses during the Great War, when the officers came round. The officers always gave good money for a horse but sometimes the horses were like brothers and the men couldn't let them go, so they hid them. I wasn't called up. Nothing happened to me and I didn't remind them. We didn't really miss the men who didn't come back. The village stayed the same. If there were changes, I never felt them, so I can't remark on them. There was still no money about. People seemed to live without it. They also lived without the Church. I'm sorry about this but it's true. I hardly ever went when I was young. The holy time was the harvest. Just before it began, the farmer would call his men together and say, 'Tell me your harvest bargain.' So the men chose a harvest lord who told the farmer how much they wanted to get the harvest in, and then master and lord shook hands on the bargain.

We reaped by hand. You could count thirty mowers in the same field, each followed by his partner, who did the sheaving. The mowers used their own scythes and were very particular about them. They cost 7s. 6d. in Wickham Market, but it wasn't the buying of them, it was the keeping them sharp. You would get a man who could never learn to sharpen, no matter how he tried. A mate might help him, but then he might not. Some men mowed so quick they just fled through the corn all the day long. Each mower took eleven rows of corn on his blade, no more and no less. We were allowed seventeen pints of beer a day each and none of this beer might leave the field once it had been bought. What was left each day had to be kept and drunk before eight on a Saturday night . . .

The lord sat atop of the last load to leave the field and then the women and children came to glean the stubble. Master would then kill a couple of sheep for the Horkey supper and afterwards we all went shouting home. Shouting in the empty old fields – I don't know why. But that's what we did. We'd shout so loud that the boys in the next village would shout back . . .

(from *Akenfield: Portrait of an English Village,* 1960)

The Shepherd

How sweet is the shepherd's sweet lot!
From the morn to the evening he strays;
He shall follow his sheep all the day,
And his tongue shall be fillèd with praise.

For he hears the lambs' innocent call
And he hears the ewes' tender reply;
He is watchful; while they are in peace,
For they know when their shepherd is nigh.

WILLIAM BLAKE

*

The Waggon-Maker

I have made tales in verse, but this man made
Waggons of elm to last a hundred years;
The blacksmith forged the rims and iron gears,
His was the magic that the wood obeyed.

Each deft device that country wisdom bade,
Or farmers' practice needed, he preserved.
He wrought the subtle contours, straight and curved,
Only by eye, and instinct of the trade.

No weakness, no offence in any part,
It stood the strain in mired fields and roads
In all a century's struggle for its bread;
Bearing, perhaps, eight thousand heavy loads,
Beautiful always as a work of art,
Homing the bride, and harvest, and men dead.

JOHN MASEFIELD

In the Forest

WALTER DE LA MARE

While my father was away at the war, I marked off each day
with my knife on a piece of wood. He had started when it was
scarcely light beneath the trees. I was very sleepy so early in
the morning while he ate his breakfast, and as I watched him
on the other side of the lighted candle drinking his steaming
tea in his saucer, my eyes kept rolling back of themselves because I was so tired. And everything in the room was plain
one moment and the next all blurred and wavering. The baby
was asleep in the cradle. The wind was still roaring in the
tops of the trees, but the candle burned clear, because the
wind did not come down into the house.

When my father opened the door I saw that the grass was
strewn with green leaves, and falling leaves were in the air,
and the wind overhead sounded like water, though the tree-
trunks hardly swayed even, down here. But it was not raining
when he started, only the leaves were wet with rain and the
bark of the trees was darkened with wet. I asked him to bring
me back a long rifle. He kept rubbing his hands over his face
and blinking his eyes and listening to the wind as if he heard
the guns. Two or three times he came back to say good-bye
to my mother. And even when at last he didn't come back he
kept turning his face, looking over his shoulder at us. There
was no sun shining yet that morning, but the bright light of
the sky gleamed on the wet leaves. I asked mother if
father was glad to be going to the war. But she was crying
over the baby, so I went out into the forest till dinner.

My mother was more cheerful at dinner, and we had some
hot soup. After dinner I chopped up some wood in the shed.
It made me very hot and excited chopping up the wood. It
was getting dark when I came back, carrying the logs. It
seemed that the wind grew more angry in the twilight, and
although it still roared like the mill-water in the village, yet
it whistled too, and the leaves kept dropping, heavy with rain.

And now it was not clear, but cold and misty round the hut. I went in with the logs.

Mother was sitting in the wooden chair with the baby in her arms. She looked as if she was pretending. I went close and stared at her, and found that she was fast asleep. The baby was asleep too, but it scarcely seemed to be really breathing – it was like a moth fluttering on a pin; its face was quite pale and still in its sleep, but its cheeks were very red. I thought I would make a fire again without asking my mother's leave, so as to be more cheerful; besides, I could feel the cold air oozing through the crannies of the timbers, and it was getting so dark I could see only the white things in the room. The rushing sound of the wind never ceased at all.

As soon as the flames began to spring up, and the sparks to crack out of the wood, my mother woke up. She looked at me with a curious face; but soon she remembered that she had been asleep, and she enjoyed the warmth of the fire.

On the next day I woke up where I had fallen asleep by the hearth, and it was a very quiet morning. I looked out of the window, and saw the sun shining yellow between the branches; and many of the boughs were now all but bare. But the fallen leaves lay thick on the ground as far as I could see, and some of them were still quite large and green. I was glad my father was gone away, because now I could do just as I pleased. I did not want the trouble of lighting the fire, so I went out into the forest, and down to visit the snares. There was a young hare caught by the leg in one, and the leaves were all round him. His eyes were bleeding, and not very bright. I killed him with a crack on the neck as I had seen father kill the hares, and carried him back by his hind legs. The leaves made an incessant rustling as I walked through them. I could see the blue sky above the trees; it was very pale, like a ribbon. I stood still a minute, carrying the hare, and listening to find if I could hear the guns. But I heard only a bird singing and a rushing sound, as if a snake were going away under the leaves. Sometimes I came to branches blown down to the ground, and even now, here and there, a leaf would fall slowly through the air, twirling, to be with all the

214

rest. I enjoyed my broth for dinner very much, and the hare lasted for three days, with some turnips.

I asked mother how long father would be away. She said she could not tell. And I wondered how they would carry back his body if he was killed in the war.

I stayed out in the forest nearly all that day because the baby kept on crying. It was dark, and the window was lit up when I came home, and still the baby was fretting. Its eyes were gone dull, and it would not go to sleep in the night, though mother kept walking up and down, crooning and mumbling to it, and rocking it in her arms. She said it was very ill, and she held it pressed close to her. I asked her if it was going to die, but she only walked a little faster, and, as I was very sleepy, we did not talk much that night. The baby was still crying when I woke up, but not so loud. It was bleating small and shrill; like a young lamb, I told mother. I felt very refreshed after my sleep, and very hungry. I lit the fire and boiled the kettle, and put the plates on the table, and the loaf.

After breakfast I told mother I was going down to the old pool to fish, and that I would bring her some fish for dinner. But she looked at me and called me to her.

'The baby is dreadfully ill,' she said, 'and we must go without the fish. Feel its poor thin hot hands. That's the fever. Do you love it? Then take it in your arms.'

But I shook my head. It looked very ugly because its face was all puckered up, and it just wailed and wailed like a gnat in the air.

'I think I would like to go fishing, mother,' I said, 'and I promise you shall have the biggest I catch.'

But she kept on persisting that the baby was too ill to wait, that it was very queer, and that I must go for the doctor in the village. It wasn't so very far, she said, and I could fish tomorrow.

'But it is far,' I told her; 'and it doesn't look so very bad; and it might be windy and cold tomorrow. It's only crying,' I said. And I ran out before she could catch me.

But I did not catch any fish. I supposed they would not bite because I had been wicked. So I tied up my lines and came home about three in the afternoon. As I stood at the door waiting before going in, I heard a sound far away, and then, in a while, again, through the forest. And I knew it was the guns and cannons on the other side of the forest. The baby was not crying now, when I went in. But my mother did not turn her head to speak to me. She was kneeling beside its old rocking-cradle, some of her hair hanging down on her shoulders.

'I'll go for the doctor now, mother; but the guns are firing; you can hear them now if you come and listen at the door.'

But when I told her about the guns, she began to cry out loud, and hid her face in the coverlet on the cradle. I watched her a little while, and I could hear the cannons going off quite plainly now; only far away, like a drum when you put your hand on it.

I got very hot standing still, so I put my tackle on the hook and sat down by the hearth.

216

'Shall I go for the doctor now, mother? It'll be dark before I get back.'

Mother turned on me very wild. 'Oh, you coward, you coward!' she said. 'Dark – it's dark enough for me!'

She startled me very much by saying this and I felt very uncomfortable. I went nearer and looked, The baby's face was white, and its eyelids were like white wax. Its lips were the colour of its hands, almost blue.

'Is it dead, mother?' I asked. But she did not answer me, only shook her shoulders. I walked away and looked out of the door. First I felt hot and then my back shivered. And I began to cry too, because I had not gone in the morning for the doctor. I did not dry my eyes because the tears ran quite hot down my cheeks, and I could hear them dripping off my chin upon my jacket. I liked to have the door open, although it was cold and grey in the afternoon.

My mother came to the doorway and drew me close to her as if she were sorry, with her hand clutching my head. I could not cry any more now, but stood still; and even then the guns and cannons went on firing. And sometimes birds flew silently between the trees away from the sound. I wondered if father was fighting near the cannons.

The next day it was so cold again my mother made me a jacket out of an old coat of father's. It was just hemmed up, and I wore it instead of my other jacket when I went out. She had drawn the coverlet over the baby's face, so that it now lay in a kind of little house in its cradle. I thought I would please mother, so found the place and read out of the Bible about Herod; but the candle burned very sooty and smoky, so that I could not read very well, and left out the long words.

The next morning mother told me to go down to the village and tell the sexton that the baby was dead so that it could be buried in the churchyard.

I started out with my switch, about ten o'clock. It was a warm day; so I was wearing my old jacket again, and the air smelled of the leaves, which were withered and yellow and brown. I went on, whistling; but it was more than five miles to the village. The robins were singing on the twigs, and I saw some crows flying in the sky. It was so quiet in the forest, that the cannons seemed to shake the air with their sound.

And while I was walking along, not very fast, and looking out for wild berries, I heard a noise in the distance of men running, and then the sound of a rifle quite near, and a scream like a rabbit, but much more loud and awful. I hid behind a tree, and when the forest was quiet again I ran home as quick as I could. But I did not like to tell mother that I had been frightened of the soldiers, because she had called me a coward already. So I said instead that the sexton was nowhere to be found in the village, that he must have gone to the war himself, and that no one would come for fear of the soldiers.

She looked me full in the face with her eyes. She looked so earnestly and so hard at me that I could not help moving my shoulder a little. And at that she turned away, and I felt very wretched because I knew that she had seen it was a lie. But I did not say anything.

All the while I sat there my eyes would not keep from looking at the cradle. I was very hungry. But since mother was putting on her shawl I knew that she was going out presently. Then, I thought, when she is gone, I will eat as much as ever I can. There were some bones in the cupboard well worth picking, I knew. When mother had put on her shawl and her bonnet, she lifted the baby out of the cradle.

'I must carry it to the churchyard myself,' she said, but more to herself than to me. There were no tears in her eyes; they were dark all round.

'Won't you kiss your little brother, Robbie?' It was wrapped up in her wedding shawl, which she had sometimes shown me of an evening, out of the chest. I began to cry when I kissed its forehead. It was as cold as a stone, as a piece of dough, and looked very heavy, yet thin, and its face was quite still now.

'Take care of the house, Rob,' she said. 'Don't go out; and bolt the door after me.'

I watched her hasten off along the narrow path between the trees. There was a light like crimson in the forest, and I knew that the sun would soon be setting. It was silly of her not to have gone earlier. It was very quiet now; and I was afraid it would soon be dark.

Soon she was out of sight, and only the trees seemed to come a little nearer and stand still. I left the door open, went into the room and put the candlestick on the table. I kicked the log till it began to flame. Then I went to the cupboard and took out the loaf and the bones, and a few puckered old apples. I ate from the dish, sitting by the hearth, looking out of the door. When I had finished I fell asleep for a little while.

By and by I opened my eyes. It was darker, and I saw some animal looking in at the door. I jumped up, and the animal ran away. Then I shut and barred the door and put some more wood on the fire until it was blazing high up the chimney. But I did not like to look over my shoulder towards the square window; it was dark and silent and watchful out there. I could not hear the cannons now, either because they weren't sounding or because the flames made a loud bubbling noise as they ran up and waved. I did not dare to let them fall quiet, to only the red embers, so I kept on putting wood on the fire as fast as it burned away.

Mother did not come back, and it seemed I was sitting in front of the warm hearth in a dream that would never come to an end. All was still and motionless, and there was no ordinary sound at all that I could hear in the forest, and even the cannons were more muffled now and farther away. I could not cry, though I felt very angry at being left alone, and I was afraid. Besides, I didn't know what I would say to mother when she came back – about the food. Yet I longed for her too, and got a pain with it, and felt that I loved her, and was very sorry for my wickedness.

I fell asleep unawares. When I awoke it was broad daylight. I felt very glad and relieved to see the light, even though mother had not come back. It seemed to me that some noise had awakened me. Presently there came a groan at the doorway. Kneeling down and peeping through a crevice between the planks, I saw my father lying there on the door step. I took down the bar and opened the door. He was lying on his stomach; his clothes were filthy and torn, and at the back of his shoulder was a small hole pushed in in the cloth. There was dark, thick blood on the withered leaves. I tried to see his face, but couldn't very well. It was all muddy, bleared and white, and he groaned and swore when I touched him. But he didn't know who I was, and some of what he said didn't seem to me to have any sense.

He asked for some water, but I could not turn him over so that he could drink it. And it was all spilt. I told him about the baby dying, but he didn't show that he could hear anything; and just as I finished I heard mother coming back from the churchyard. So I ran out and told her that it was father.

(from *The Wind Blows Over*, 1936)

ENCHANTMENT

I Know a Bank whereon the
Wild Thyme Blows

I know a bank whereon the wild thyme blows,
Where oxlips and the nodding violet grows;
Quite over-canopied with luscious woodbine,
With sweet musk-roses, and with eglantine;
There sleeps Titania sometime of the night,
Lull'd in these flowers with dances and delight;
And there the snake throws her enamell'd skin,
Weed wide enough to wrap a fairy in . . .

(from *A Midsummer Night's Dream*) WILLIAM SHAKESPEARE

Lady into Fox

DAVID GARNETT

Often enough in classic times, gods and goddesses, nymphs and sprites were transformed into beasts of one sort or another, or into fountains, or into trees – as Apollo saw his Daphne. Here, however, is a story of a man and his wife who lived a little less than a hundred years ago.

Mr Tebrick, a gentle and pious and rich young man, married the charming Silvia Fox and took her to live in the country on his comfortable estate. And Silvia loved the country, save for one thing. She could not abide a hunt, and refused to ride to hounds – though she had done so as a child and been blooded, which had greatly upset her.

One day, walking with her husband, she heard the hounds and the horn and the hunt streamed by not far away. Mr Tebrick was anxious to see them, and caught his wife by the hand, pulling her to a vantage point. She struggled and hung back. Then suddenly she gave a piercing cry, so that he turned in alarm. *Where his wife had been the moment before was a small fox, of a very bright red . . .*

(The distraught husband takes his wife home, and they live as best they can . . . But the time comes when she leaves him for the wild.

One morning, Mr Tebrick hears a fox bark, and he rushes out, hoping it may be Silvia . . .)

*

The sun was not yet high, the dew thick everywhere, and for a minute or two everything was very silent. He looked about him eagerly but could see no fox, yet there was already joy in his heart.

Then while he looked up and down the road, he saw his vixen step out of the copse about thirty yards away. He called to her at once.

'My dearest wife! Oh, Silvia! You are come back!' and at the sound of his voice he saw her wag her tail, which set his last doubts at rest.

But then though he called her again, she stepped into the copse once more though she looked back at him over her shoulder as she went. At this he ran after her, but softly and not too fast lest he should frighten her away, and then looked about for her again and called to her when he saw her among the trees still keeping her distance from him. He followed her then, and as he approached so she retreated from him, yet always looking back at him several times.

He followed after her through the underwood up the side of the hill, when suddenly she disappeared from his sight, behind some bracken.

When he got there he could see her nowhere, but looking about him found a fox's earth, but so well hidden that he might have passed it by a thousand times and would never have found it unless he had made particular search at that spot.

But now, though he went on his hands and knees, he could see nothing of his vixen, so that he waited a little while wondering.

Presently he heard a noise of something moving in the earth, and so waited silently, then saw something which pushed itself into sight. It was a small sooty black beast, like a puppy. Then came another behind it, then another and so on till there were five of them. Lastly there came his vixen pushing her litter before her, and while he looked at her silently, a prey to his confused and unhappy emotions, he saw that her eyes were shining with pride and happiness.

She picked up one of her youngsters then, in her mouth, and brought it to him and laid it in front of him, and then looked up at him very excited, or so it seemed.

Mr Tebrick took the cub in his hands, stroked it and put it against his cheek. It was a little fellow with a smutty face and paws, with staring vacant eyes of a brilliant electric blue and a little tail like a carrot. When he was put down he took a step towards his mother and then sat down very comically.

Mr Tebrick looked at his wife again and spoke to her,

calling her a good creature. Already he was resigned and now, indeed, for the first time he thoroughly understood what had happened to her, and how far apart they were now. But looking first at one cub, then at another, and having them sprawling over his lap, he forgot himself, only watching the pretty scene, and taking pleasure in it. Now and then he would stroke his vixen and kiss her, liberties which she freely allowed him. He marvelled more than ever now at her beauty; for her gentleness with the cubs and the extreme delight she took in them seemed to him then to make her more lovely than before. Thus lying amongst them at the mouth of the earth he idled away the whole of the morning . . .

(Mr Tebrick becomes very fond of his wife's family, calls himself their godfather and gives them all names. He spends many lovely weeks in the woods with them. Then suddenly they are no longer

*dependent pups, but set out hunting. Mr Tebrick is determined to
keep up with them . . .)*

Mr Tebrick now could follow after them anywhere and
keep up with them, too, and could go through a wood as
silently as a deer. He learnt to conceal himself if ever a
labourer passed by so that he was rarely seen, and never but
once in their company. But what was most strange of all, he
had got a way of going doubled up, often almost on all fours
with his hands touching the ground every now and then,
particularly when he went up hill.

He hunted with them, too, sometimes, chiefly by coming
up and scaring rabbits towards where the cubs lay ambushed,
so that the bunnies ran straight into their jaws.

He was useful to them in other ways, climbing up and
robbing pigeons' nests for the eggs which they relished
exceedingly, or by occasionally dispatching a hedgehog for
them so they did not get the prickles in their mouths. But
while on his part he thus altered his conduct, they on their
side were not behindhand, but learnt a dozen human tricks
from him that are ordinarily wanting in Reynard's education.

One evening he went to a cottager who had a row of skeps,
and bought one of them, just as it was after the man had
smothered the bees. This he carried to the foxes that they
might taste the honey, for he had seen them dig out wild
bees' nests often enough. The skep full was indeed a wonderful feast for them, they bit greedily into the heavy scented
comb, their jaws were drowned in the sticky flood of sweet-
ness, and they gorged themselves on it without restraint.
When they had munched up the last morsel they tore the
skep in pieces, and for hours afterwards they were happily
employed in licking themselves clean.

That night he slept near their lair, but they left him and
went hunting. In the morning when he woke he was quite
numb with cold, and faint with hunger. A white mist hung
over everything and the wood smelt of autumn.

He got up and stretched his cramped limbs, and then
walked homewards. The summer was over and Mr Tebrick
noticed this now for the first time and was astonished. He

reflected that the cubs were fast growing up, they were foxes at all points, and yet when he thought of the time when they had been sooty and had blue eyes it seemed to him only yesterday. From that he passed to thinking of the future, asking himself as he had done once before what would become of his vixen and her children. Before the winter he must tempt them into the security of his garden and fortify it against all the dangers that threatened them . . .

[Alas, the summer is indeed over. It is autumn, the beginning of the hunting season . . .]

*

The Ride-by-Nights

Up on their brooms the Witches stream,
Crooked and black in the crescent's gleam:
One foot high, and one foot low,
Bearded, cloaked, and cowled they go.
'Neath Charlie's Wane they twitter and tweet,
And away they swarm 'neath the Dragon's feet.
With a whoop and a flutter they swing and sway,
And surge pell-mell down the Milky Way.
Betwixt the legs of the glittering Chair
They hover and squeak in the empty air.
Then round they swoop past the glimmering Lion
To where Sirius barks behind huge Orion:
Up, then, and over to wheel amain,
Under the silver, and home again.

WALTER DE LA MARE

Witches' Spell

FIRST WITCH
Thrice the brinded cat hath mew'd.
SECOND WITCH
Thrice and once the hedge-pig whined.
THIRD WITCH
Harpier cries ' 'Tis time, 'tis time.'
FIRST WITCH
Round about the cauldron go:
In the poison'd entrails throw.
Toad, that under cold stone
Days and nights has thirty one
Swelter'd venom sleeping got,
Boil thou first i' the charmed pot.

ALL

Double, double toil and trouble;
Fire burn and cauldron bubble.

SECOND WITCH

Fillet of a fenny snake,
In the cauldron boil and bake;
Eye of newt and toe of frog,
Wool of bat and tongue of dog,
Adder's fork and blind-worm's sting,
Lizard's leg and owlet's wing,
For a charm of powerful trouble,
Like a hell-broth boil and bubble.

ALL

Double, double toil and trouble;
Fire burn and cauldron bubble.

THIRD WITCH

Scale of dragon, tooth of wolf,
Witches' mummy, maw and gulf
Of the ravin'd salt-sea shark,
Root of hemlock digg'd i' the dark;
Liver of blaspheming Jew,
Gall of goat and slips of yew
Sliver'd in the moon's eclipse,
Nose of Turk and Tartar's lips,
Finger of birth-strangled babe
Ditch-deliver'd by a drab,
Make the gruel thick and slab:
Add thereto a tiger's chaudron,
For the ingredients of our cauldron.

ALL

Double, double toil and trouble;
Fire burn and cauldron bubble.

SECOND WITCH

Cool it with a baboon's blood,
Then the charm is firm and good . . .

(from *Macbeth*) WILLIAM SHAKESPEARE

A Witches' Sabbath in the English Countryside

SYLVIA TOWNSEND WARNER

A respectable maiden aunt may or may not seem a suitable candidate for witchdom. Miss Laura Willowes – Aunt Lolly – has always known that some unusual turn of fate lies ahead of her. Free at last of the demands of relations, she takes up residence in the village of Great Mop, where she is soon involved in curious developments. Escorted by her landlady, Mrs Leak, she attends a Witches' Sabbath, finding there many other apparently ordinary village residents . . .

*

They walked down the road in silence as far as the milestone, and turned into the track that went up the hillside and past the wood. Others had turned that way also. The gate stood open, and voices sounded ahead. It was then that Laura guessed the truth and turned to her companion.

'Where are you taking me?' she said. Mrs Leak made no answer, but in the darkness she took hold of Laura's hand. There was no need of further explanation. They were going to the Witches' Sabbath. Mrs Leak was a witch, too; a matronly witch like Agnes Sampson [*who was a real witch*], she would be Laura's chaperone. The night was full of voices. Padding rustic footsteps went by them in the dark. When they had reached the brow of the hill a faint continuous sound, resembling music, was borne towards them by the light wind . . .

The meeting-place was some way off, by the time they reached it Laura's eyes had grown accustomed to the darkness. She could see a crowd of people walking about in a large field; lights of some sort were burning under a hedge, and one or two paper garlands were looped over the trees. When she first caught sight of them, the assembled witches and warlocks seemed to be dancing, but now the music had stopped and they were just walking about . . . [*It is now that Laura meets various neighbours.*]

Then a young man whom she did not know came up to Laura and put his arm respectfully round her waist. She found herself expected to dance. She could not hear any music, but she danced as best she could, keeping time to the rhythm of his breath upon her cheek. Their dance was short; she supposed she had not acquitted herself to her partner's satisfaction, for after a few turns he released her, and left her standing by the hedge. Not a word had passed between them. Laura felt that she ought to say something, but she could not think of a suitable opening. It was scarcely possible to praise the floor.

A familiar discouragement began to settle upon her spirits. In spite of her hopes, she was not going to enjoy herself. Even as a witch, it seemed, she was doomed to social failure, and her first Sabbath was not going to open livelier vistas than her first ball . . . [*Then, later –*]

The Sabbath was warming up nicely now, everyone was jigging it, even Laura. For a while Mrs Leak kept up a semblance of chaperonage. Suddenly appearing at Laura's elbow she would ask her if she were enjoying herself, and glancing at her would slip away before she could answer. Or with vague gestures she indicated some evasively bowing partner, male or female; and silently Laura would give her hand and be drawn into the dance, presently to be relinquished or carried off by someone else.

The etiquette of a Sabbath appeared to consist of one rule only: to do nothing for long. Partners came and went, figures and conformations were in a continual flux. Sometimes the dancers were coupled, sometimes they jigged in a circle round some specially agile performer, sometimes they all took hands and galloped about the field. Halfway through a very formal quadrille presided over by the Misses Larpent they fell abruptly to playing Fox and Geese. In spite of Mr Gurdon's rosette there was no Master of Ceremonies. A single mysterious impulse seemed to govern the company. They wheeled and manoeuvred like a flock of starlings.

After an hour or two of this Laura felt dizzy and bewildered. Taking advantage of the general lack of formality she tore herself from Mr Gurdon's arms, not to dance with another, but to slip away and sit quietly in the hedge.

She wondered where the music came from. She had heard it quite clearly as she came over the hill, but upon entering the field she had lost it. Now as she watched the others she heard it once more. When they neared it grew louder, when they retreated into the darkness it faded with them, as though the sound issued from the dancers themselves, and hung, a droning exhalation, above their heads. It was an odd kind of music, a continuous high shapeless blurr of sound. It was something like mosquitoes in a hot bedroom, and something like a distant threshing machine. But beside this, it had a faintly human quality, a metallic breathing as of trombones marking the measure; and when the dancers took hands and revolved in a leaping circle the music leaped and pounded with them, so much like the steam-organ music of a merry-go-round that for a moment Laura thought that they were riding on horses and dragons, bobbing up and down on crested dragons with heads like cocks, and horses with blood-red nostrils.

The candles burnt on in the dry ditch. Though the boughs of the thorn-trees moved above them and grated in the night-wind, the candle flames flowed steadily upwards. Thus lit from below, the dancers seemed of more than human stature, their bodies extending into the darkness as if in emulation of their gigantic upcast shadows. The air was full of the smell of bruised grass . . .

[*Thus Laura sits watching a long while; but then –*]

She was roused by a shrill whistle. The others heard it too. Miss Minnie and Miss Jane scrambled up and hurried across the field, outdistancing Mrs Dewey, who followed them panting for breath and twitching her skirts over the rough ground. The music had stopped. Laura saw all the witches and warlocks jostling each other and pressing into a circle. She won-

232

dered what was happening now. Whatever it was, it seemed to please and excite them a great deal, for she could hear them all laughing and talking at once. Some newcomer, she supposed – for their behaviour was that of a welcome. Now the newcomer must be making a speech, for they all became silent; a successful speech, for the silence was broken by acclamations and bursts of laughter.

'Of course!' said Laura. 'It must be Satan!'

(from *Lolly Willowes*, 1926)

Daphne and Apollo

When Apollo, god of the sun, therefore of life itself, slew the great serpent, Python, there was much rejoicing on the slopes of Mount Parnassus. The beast had terrorized the countryside, and there was no praise too high for its slayer. Apollo was as proud of himself as they were, but with becoming modesty assured his grateful admirers that it was his fine great bow, his fiery arrows that had brought success to his venture.

'So fine an exploit should be commemorated!' they cried. 'What shall we do to honour Apollo, our strength and our saviour?'

Apollo decided to institute games, to be known as the Pythian Games – which would satisfactorily perpetuate the tale of the god's achievement.

'The victor,' pronounced Apollo, 'shall be crowned with a wreath of fine beech leaves.'

Like any other young man, god or not, vain of his own prowess, Apollo was impatient of rivals. Even the sight of Venus's boy, Cupid, playing with a bow and arrows of his own, was distasteful to him.

'You are too young for such warlike weapons, boy! To bend the bow is an art you can hardly understand. Then leave it to stronger hands.'

'I am not setting out to slaughter fiery monsters, Apollo,' Cupid replied. 'My bow is a small bow – but my arrows are unlike yours. They find a different mark – but they are as powerful in their way.'

'Tush, now, my child,' said Apollo, grown irritated by the lad's lack of respect. 'Lay by your bow, forget your arrows. These are *my* weapons, *my* strength and *my* distinction . . . I trust you have understood what I have been saying?'

Cupid turned away, muttering crossly under his breath, 'My arrows may not strike and kill great scaly monsters with fiery breath – yet one shall strike you, Apollo.'

It was not the lad's intention to shoot to kill – indeed, his arrows sped on their way with quite a different intention. They were of two sorts: one bright gold and sharp-pointed, the other blunt and tipped with lead. The gold arrow, when it pierced its quarry, caused an access of passionate and overpowering love to centre on the next creature of the opposite sex that the victim came upon. The lead-tipped arrow induced the exact opposite emotion – a fever of revulsion.

Cupid, by no means as young and foolish as Apollo might like to believe, knew well that the god was already more than half in love with the delightful nymph Daphne. She was the daughter of Peneus, the river god, much courted by lovers of all conditions – some bold, some sighing; some young and handsome, some inclining towards the baldness of middle-age. Daphne remained aloof and indifferent to these many protestations of love and devotion. Her own devotion was to the Goddess Diana; like Diana, it was Daphne's intention to remain chaste until her dying day.

'You must surely grant me this, dearest father,' she often cried to Peneus. 'Let me keep my virginity!'

'You owe me grandchildren!' he grumbled in reply. 'Must I go short of a son-in-law to aid my advancing years? Besides – what nonsense is this? You are too beautiful not to inspire love, and one day love must of a certainty become your own inspiration.'

But she shook her head, insisting she would remain a faithful votaress of Diana, the Queen of Heaven.

Apollo spent long hours on the woody fringe of the forest, waiting for a mere glimpse of Daphne, and there Cupid, too, might be found. And one day as Daphne was seen approaching, Cupid shot from his bow twice – the golden, piercing arrow of love he sent straight to its mark somewhere in the region of Apollo's heart; the blunt arrow, tipped with lead, struck Daphne.

Immediately, there came a dramatic and alarming change in both Cupid's victims. Apollo's passion of love swept uncontrollably through his whole being. He was consumed with desire for Daphne, while she, who had merely tried to ignore him, was now seized with a most terrible and overruling distaste. She fled – he followed. She had never seemed

235

so enchanting in his eyes. Her familiar blushes that changed to pallor; her golden hair streaming over her shoulders as the braid slipped out of place; her shoulders and arms deliciously displayed as haste brought dishevelment . . . Ah, if so much as he could see of her exercised such an enchantment over him, how would it be when the last concealment of her beauty fell away?

'How shall I live, unless she is entirely mine?' Apollo gasped out loud as he ran. 'She is the most truly heavenly creature I have ever seen!' And he called after her, finding breath enough even though he was moving so fast and fleet – 'Stay! Stay, divine girl! Do not flee – stay! I am no wolf, no hawk! I am the god Apollo, and your devoted slave!'

But on she went, for Apollo the son of Jupiter could hold no delight for her; this handsome god of music and piping meant far less than the meanest, ugliest peasant too humble to raise his eyes to her beautiful face . . .

The forest echoed with Apollo's cries as Daphne fled before him. Trees and flowers swayed and shivered with the speed of their passing, the violence of their emotion. By the very nature of things, the hunter was bound to gain on his weaker quarry. Daphne began to falter. Ahead of her was home, the river where her father held sway. As she strained towards that place her breathing grew ever more painful. She was ready to sink to the ground – and would willingly have done so had she been certain of instant death's embrace, rather than the embraces of Apollo. In despair, at her last gasp, Daphne cried out for help to her father – to Peneus, the river God.

'Help me dearest father!' the poor girl cried weakly. 'Let the ground open to swallow me! Let the waters close over my head! Only save me! Or change me, father – give me some other form than this human form that has been my ruin!'

Peneus heard her cries and exerted all his powers to help her, though by doing so he lost for ever the daughter he loved, the grandchildren he craved.

Daphne slowed and faltered. A strange stiffness took her limbs. Her feet no longer carried her, but remained as if rooted to the ground. Her arms, so supple and so delicately rounded, began to change their shape. It was as though a garment of leaves and twigs were flung over her, and into its folds there vanished her hands, her face, her hair . . .

Before Apollo's eyes, his beautiful nymph Daphne was transformed into a small and shapely tree, its dark glossy leaves catching the sunlight, as the breeze gently moved them in the sheltered forest glade that ran down to the riverside.

Groaning, the god fell upon his knees, caught at the branches, embraced the trunk, kissed the leaves. Tears of remorse and wretchedness poured from his eyes.

'Daphne! Daphne! What has come to you? How shall I endure this parting? You can never be my wife now!' He grovelled about the roots of the pretty tree, as if he were kissing his nymph's delicious feet. 'I shall never forget you!' he cried, 'I shall never cease to honour you. By my godhead I proclaim it – your leaves shall never wither, but shall remain green and young through the bitterest winter.'

Thereafter, Apollo took the laurel, the tree into which his Daphne had been transformed, for his own emblem. He adorned his lyre with laurel leaves, and bound them about his brow. He decreed that the victor of the Pythian games should be crowned, not as previously decided with fresh beech leaves, but with a chaplet of laurel. And so, in the future, would emperors be crowned, and ever after through the years the laurel should stand as a tribute to victory . . .

So, indeed, it has happened; though it is doubtful that the laurel-crowned victor of our times remembers Daphne and Apollo as he accepts the tribute.

Traditional

The Ghost Chase

What sight is this? . . . on dazzling snow,
Cold as a shroud beneath the sky,
Swoop into view, the valley through,
Fox, horsemen, hounds – in soundless cry!
Hulla! Hullo! Hulla-hoo!

Reynard himself, muzzle to brush,
Is whiter than the crystal track
He races over in the hush
Of woods that cast no rumour back.

The voiceless hounds are white as he;
Huntsman and horse – no scarlet theirs;
No fleck, mark, dapple, or spot to see,
White as the North, horses and mares.

They move as in a dream – no stir,
No hoof-fall, music, tongue or steel –
Swift as a noiseless scimitar
Cutting the snows the winds congeal.

Now they are gone. O Dove-white yews!
O sleep-still vale! All silent lies
The calm savanna of the snows,
Beneath the blue of arctic skies!
Hulla! Hullo! Hulla-hoo!

WALTER DE LA MARE

Pan With Us

Pan came out of the woods one day —
His skin and his hair and his eyes were grey,
The grey of the moss of walls were they —
    And stood in the sun and looked his fill
    At wooded valley and wooded hill.

He stood in the zephyrs, pipes in hand,
On a height of naked pasture land;
In all the country he did command
    He saw no smoke and he saw no roof.
    That was well! and he stamped a hoof.

His heart knew peace, for none came here
To this lean feeding save once a year
Someone to salt the half-wild steer,
    Or homespun children with clicking pails
    Who see so little they tell no tales.

He tossed his pipes, too hard to teach
A new-world song, far out of reach,
For a sylvan sign that the blue jay's screech
    And the whimper of hawks beside the sun
    Were music enough for him, for one.

Times were changed from what they were:
Such pipes kept less of power to stir
The fruited bough of the juniper
    And the fragile bluets clustered there
    Than the merest aimless breath of air.

They were pipes of pagan mirth,
And the world had found new terms of worth.
He laid him down on the sun-burned earth
    And ravelled a flower and looked away —
    Play? Play? — What should he play?

ROBERT FROST

The Knight's Story

MARY MACGREGOR

Sheltering in the poor fisherman's cottage, the knight, Huldbrand, tells of his fearful journey through the dread forest. Beside him sits Undine, the fisherman's foster-child, herself, though they do not know it, a creature from the spirit world . . .

*

'It must be about eight days now,' said the knight, 'since I left my castle of Ringstetten, and journeyed towards the city that lies beyond the haunted forest.

'The city was gay with lords and ladies who had come thither for the tournament which was then being held.

'I at once entered the lists, for my steed was strong and I myself was eager for the fray. Once, as I rested from the combat, my eyes fell upon a lady who was wondrous fair. She was looking down from a gallery upon the tournament.

'Bertalda was the name of the beautiful maiden, and she was the foster-child of a great duke. I knew that, as I again seized my lance, the lady's eyes followed me into the lists, and I fought even more bravely than before.

'In the evening a great festival was held, and here I met Bertalda and danced with her; indeed, evening after evening we were together until the tournament drew to a close.'

As Huldbrand spoke these words he felt a sharp pain in his left hand. It was hanging by his side, and as he looked down to see what had caused the pain, he found that Undine had fastened in it her little pearly teeth.

The knight could see that the maiden's face was no longer smiling. She looked up at him and there was sorrow in her large blue eyes as she whispered, 'Sir Knight, it is your own fault that I hurt you. I would not have you praise the lady

241

Bertalda.' Then quickly, as though ashamed of her words, she hid her face in her hands.

As the knight went on with his story, his face was grave.

'It is true,' he said, 'that Bertalda was a lovely maiden, yet as I knew her better I found her ways were cold and proud. She pleased me less as the days passed by, though, as she looked upon me with favour, I begged that as a token of it she would give me a glove.

' "You shall have it," answered she, "if you will go alone through the forest which men say is haunted, and bring me tidings of all that happens to you."

'I cared little for her glove, but would not tarry to be asked a second time to go through the forest, lest the lady should doubt my courage.'

'I thought Bertalda had loved you,' cried Undine, 'yet then had she not driven you from her into the haunted forest.'

The knight smiled at the maiden's words and then went on with the tale.

'It was but yesterday morning that I set forth on my adventure. The sun shone bright, so bright that it was not easy to believe that evil was lurking in the shadows beneath the rustling leaves. "I shall soon return," I said to myself, as I plunged into the green shade.

'But amid the maze of trees it was not long ere I lost sight of the path by which I had entered the wood.

' "It may be that I shall lose myself in this mighty forest," I thought, "but no other danger threatens me."

'I gazed up toward the sun, which had risen higher now than when first I entered the wood, and as I gazed I saw a black thing among the branches of a leafy oak.

'Was it a bear, I wondered, and my hand felt for the sword that hung at my side.

'But it was no bear, for ere long I heard a voice mocking me with rough and cruel words. "Aha, Sir Wiseacre," said the voice, "I am breaking twigs off these tall trees, so that at midnight I may light a fire in which to roast you." Then, before I could answer, the black thing grinned at me and rustled the branches, until my steed grew restless and at length galloped away.'

Undine looked at the knight, her blue eyes sparkling as she cried, 'But indeed the wicked creature did not dare to roast you, Sir Knight!'

'In its terror,' Huldbrand continued, 'my horse dashed itself against the trees, reared and again dashed madly forward. Onward we flew, until at length I saw before me a dark abyss. Yet still I found it impossible to pull up my frightened steed.

'Then all at once a tall white man stood still directly in front of my maddened horse, which swerved aside as soon as it saw him, and in that moment I was once more master of my steed. I saw also that my deliverer was not a tall white man, as I had imagined, but a brook which shone silver in the sunlight.'

'Dear brook, I will be grateful to you for evermore,' cried Undine, clapping her hands as she spoke, in childish glee. But the fisherman shook his head and was silent.

'And now,' said the knight, 'I was anxious to hasten as quickly as possible through the forest, for it seemed to me that not only might I find it difficult to regain the pathway I had lost, but that strange beings might again startle both me and my noble steed.

'I turned my horse away from the dark chasm which lay before us, but even as I did so I found at my side a strange little man. He was uglier than any one I have seen. His nose was well nigh as large as all the rest of his body, and his mouth was so big that it stretched from one ear to the other.

'This ugly creature, as soon as he saw that I had noticed him, grinned at me, until his mouth looked even larger than before. He scraped his feet along the ground and bowed mockingly to me a thousand times.

'My horse was trembling at the sight of the strange figure, so I resolved to ride on in search of further adventure, or if I found none, to ride back to the city which I had left in the morning.

'But the ugly little man did not mean to let me escape. Quick as lightning he sprang round and stood again in front of my horse.

' "Get out of the way," I now cried in anger, "lest my steed tramples you under its feet."

'This did not seem to frighten the strange creature. He laughed in my face, and then said in a gruff voice, "You must give me gold, for it was I who turned your horse aside from yonder dark abyss."

' "Nay, what you say is not true," I answered him. "It was the silver brook that saved me and my horse from being dashed to pieces. Nevertheless, take thy gold and begone."

'As I spoke I flung a coin into the strange-shaped cap which he was holding before me, then putting spurs to my horse I rode quickly forward.

'I heard the ugly little man give a loud scream, then to my surprise there he was, running by my side, grinning and making horrible grimaces.

'My horse was galloping, and I thought I would soon get away from the little man. But it seemed impossible to go faster than he, for he took a spring, a jump, and there he was still by my side. He held up the piece of gold I had thrown to him, and in a hollow voice he cried, "It is a false coin, a false coin!"

'At length I could bear his horrible shrieks no longer. I pulled up my steed, and holding out two coins I called to him, "Take the gold, but follow me no farther!"

'Then the ugly little man began to scrape his feet and bow his head, but it was plain that he was not yet satisfied.

' "I do not wish your gold," he grumbled. "I have gold enough and to spare, as you shall soon see."

'As he spoke a strange thing happened. The beautiful green ground seemed to change into clear green glass. I looked through the glass and saw in a great cavern a group of little goblins.

'They were playing at ball, these little goblins, and I noticed that all their toys were made of silver or gold. Merry little creatures, they were, running swiftly hither and thither after the ball, nor was it easy to see whether they were standing on their heads or on their heels, or whether they were running on their hands or on their feet. No sooner was their game ended than they pelted each other with their playthings, then in a mad frolic lifted handfuls of gold dust and flung it each in the other's eyes.

'All this time the ugly little man was standing half on the ground and half within the great cavern where the tiny goblins played their games. Now I heard him call to the mischievous imps to give him handfuls of gold.

'This they did, and then he, laughing in my face, showed the gold to me ere he flung it back again into the cavern.

'Then the ugly little man called to the tiny goblins to stop their pranks and look at the coins I had given to him. When they caught sight of them they held their little sides, shaking with laughter; then all at once they turned and hissed at me.

'In spite of myself terror crept over me. Again I plunged my spurs into my horse's sides, and it dashed madly off into the midst of the forest.

'When at length the flight ended, the evening lay cool and quiet around me. A white footpath seemed to point the way which led back to the city. But each time I tried to approach it a face peered at me from between the trees. I turned to escape from this new phantom, but in vain, for whichever way I turned there was the face still staring at me.

'I grew angry and urged my horse in the direction of the shadowy face, only however to find myself drenched by a stream of white foam.

'Thus I was driven away from the white footpath, and only one way, rough and tangled, was left open to me. As soon as I began to follow it, the face, though it kept close behind, did me no further harm.

'Yet again and again I turned, hoping to find that the face had disappeared. Instead I found it closer than before, and now I could see that it belonged to a tall white man. It was true that at times the long white figure seemed to be but a wandering stream, but of this I was never sure.

'I was weary now and my horse was exhausted. It seemed useless to try any longer to force my way past the white face, so I went on riding quietly along the one path left open to me. The head of the tall man then began to nod, as though to say that at length I was doing as he wished.

'By this path I reached the end of the wood, and as the meadows and the lake came into sight the white man vanished, and I found myself standing near to your little cottage' . . .

[The story goes on to tell how Undine came to love the Knight, and how in doing so, like other legendary immortals, she acquired a human soul – with many complicated results.]

(from *Undine*)

The Way through the Woods

They shut the road through the woods
Seventy years ago.
Weather and rain have undone it again,
And now you would never know
There was once a road through the woods
Before they planted the trees.
It is underneath the coppice and heath
And the thin anemones.
Only the keeper sees
That, where the ring-dove broods,
And the badgers roll at ease,
There was once a road through the woods.

Yet, if you enter the woods
Of a summer evening late,
When the night-air cools on the trout-ringed pools
Where the otter whistles his mate,
(They fear not men in the woods,
Because they see so few)
You will hear the beat of a horse's feet,
And the swish of a skirt in the dew,
Steadily cantering through
The misty solitudes.
As though they perfectly knew
The old lost road through the woods . . .
But there is no road through the woods.

RUDYARD KIPLING

The Old Forest

J. R. R. TOLKIEN

The Old Forest *comes in the sixth chapter of the first book of*
The Lord of the Rings. *Bilbo Baggins has vanished. His
nephew, Frodo, has inherited the ring Bilbo rescued. Now he
sets out with his fellow hobbits, Pippin and Merry, the faithful
Sam in attendance, to carry the Ring from threatening danger.
They come to the Old Forest, a place of sinister reputation and
unending legend . . . 'Are the stories about it true?' asks Pippin
nervously . . . 'They do say the trees do actually move,' Merry
answers . . .*

*

The hobbits now left the tunnel-gate and rode across the wide
hollow. On the far side was a faint path leading up on to the
floor of the Forest; but it vanished as soon as it brought them
under the trees. Looking back they could see the dark line of
the Hedge through the stems of trees that were already thick
about them. Looking ahead they could see only tree-trunks of
innumerable sizes and shapes: straight or bent, twisted,
leaning, squat or slender, smooth or gnarled and branched;
and all the stems were grey or green with moss and slimy,
shaggy growths.

Merry alone seemed fairly cheerful. 'You had better lead
on and find that path,' Frodo said to him. 'Don't let us lose
one another, or forget which way the Hedge lies!'

They picked a way among the trees, and their ponies
plodded along, carefully avoiding the many writhing and
interlacing roots. There was no undergrowth. The ground
was rising steadily, and as they went forward it seemed that
the trees became taller, darker, and thicker. There was no
sound, except an occasional drip of moisture falling through
the still leaves. For the moment there was no whispering or

movement among the branches; but they all got an uncomfortable feeling that they were being watched with disapproval, deepening to dislike and even enmity. The feeling steadily grew, until they found themselves looking up quickly, or glancing back over their shoulders as if they expected a sudden blow.

There was not as yet any sign of a path, and the trees seemed constantly to bar their way. Pippin suddenly felt that he could not bear it any longer, and without warning let out a shout. 'Oi! Oi!' he cried. 'I'm not going to do anything. Just let me pass through, will you?'

The others halted, startled; but the cry fell as if muffled by a heavy curtain. There was no echo or answer though the wood seemed to become more crowded and more watchful than before.

'I should not shout, if I were you,' said Merry. 'It does more harm than good.'

Frodo began to wonder if it were possible to find a way through, and if he had been right to make the others come into this abominable wood. Merry was looking from side to side, and seemed already uncertain which way to go. Pippin noticed it. 'It has not taken you long to lose us,' he said. But at that moment Merry gave a whistle of relief and pointed ahead.

'Well, well!' he said. 'These trees *do* shift. There is the Bonfire Glade in front of us (or I hope so), but the path to it seems to have moved away!'

The light grew clearer as they went forward. Suddenly they came out of the trees and found themselves in a wide circular space. There was sky above them, blue and clear to their surprise, for down under the Forest-roof they had not been able to see the rising morning and the lifting of the mist. The sun was not, however, high enough yet to shine down into the clearing, though its light was on the tree-tops. The leaves were all thicker and greener about the edges of the glade, enclosing it with an almost solid wall. No tree grew there, only rough grass and many tall plants: stalky and faded hemlocks and wood-parsley, fireweed seeding into fluffy ashes, and rampant nettles and thistles. A dreary place: but it seemed a charming and cheerful garden after the close Forest.

The hobbits felt encouraged, and looked up hopefully at the broadening daylight in the sky. At the far side of the glade there was a break in the wall of trees, and a clear path beyond it. They could see it running on into the wood, wide in places and open above, though every now and again the trees drew in and overshadowed it with their dark boughs. Up this path they rode. They were still climbing gently, but they now went much quicker, and with better hearts; for it seemed to them that the Forest had relented, and was going to let them pass unhindered after all.

But after a while the air began to get hot and stuffy. The trees drew close again on either side, and they could no longer see far ahead. Now stronger than ever they felt again the ill-will of the wood pressing on them. So silent was it, that the fall of their ponies' hoofs, rustling on dead leaves and occasionally stumbling on hidden roots, seemed to thud in their ears. Frodo tried to sing a song to encourage them, but his voice sank to a murmur.

> 'O! Wanderers in the shadowed land
> despair not! For though dark they stand,
> all woods there be must end at last,
> and see the open sun go past:
> the setting sun, the rising sun,
> the day's end, or the day begun,
> For east or west all woods must fail . . .

Fail – even as he said the word his voice faded into silence. The air seemed heavy and the making of words wearisome. Just behind them a large branch fell from an old overhanging tree with a crash into the path. The trees seemed to close in before them.

'They do not like all that about ending and failing,' said Merry. 'I should not sing any more at present. Wait till we do get to the edge, and then we'll turn and give them a rousing chorus!'

He spoke cheerfully, and if he felt any great anxiety, he did

251

not show it. The others did not answer. They were depressed. A heavy weight was settling steadily on Frodo's heart, and he regretted now with every step forward that he had ever thought of challenging the menace of the trees. He was, indeed, just about to stop and propose going back (if that was still possible), when things took a new turn. The path stopped climbing, and became for a while nearly level. The dark trees drew aside, and ahead they could see the path going almost straight forward. Before them, but some distance off, there stood a green hill-top, treeless, rising like a bald head out of the encircling wood. The path seemed to be making directly for it.

They now hurried forward again, delighted with the thought of climbing out for a while above the roof of the Forest. The path dipped and then again began to climb upwards, leading them at last to the foot of the steep hillside. There it left the trees and faded into the turf. The wood stood all round the hill like thick hair that ended sharply in a circle round a shaven crown.

The hobbits led their ponies up, winding round and round until they reached the top. There they stood and gazed about them. The air was gleaming and sunlit, but hazy; and they could not see to any great distance. Near at hand the mist was now almost gone; though here and there it lay in the hollows of the wood, and to the south of them, out of a deep fold cutting right across the Forest, the fog still rose like steam or wisps of white smoke.

'That,' said Merry, pointing with his hand, 'that is the line of the Withywindle. It comes out of the Downs and flows south-west through the midst of the Forest to join the Brandywine below Haysend. We don't want to go *that* way! The Withywindle valley is said to be the queerest part of the whole wood – the centre from which all the queerness comes, as it were.'

The others looked in the direction Merry pointed out, but they could see little but mists over the damp and deep-cut valley; and beyond it the southern half of the Forest faded from view.

The sun on the hill-top was now getting hot. It must have

been about eleven o'clock; but the autumn haze still prevented them from seeing much in other directions. In the west they could not make out either the line of the Hedge or the valley of the Brandywine beyond it. Northward, where they looked most hopefully, they could see nothing that might be the line of the great East Road, for which they were making. They were on an island in a sea of trees, and the horizon was veiled.

On the south-eastern side the ground fell very steeply, as if the slopes of the hill were continued far down under the trees, like island-shores that really are the sides of a mountain rising out of deep waters. They sat on the green edge and looked out over the woods below them, while they ate their midday meal. As the sun rose and passed noon they glimpsed far off in the east the grey-green lines of the Downs that lay beyond the Old Forest on that side. That cheered them greatly, for it was good to see a sight of anything beyond the wood's borders, though they did not mean to go that way if they could help it: the Barrow-downs had as sinister a reputation in hobbit-legend as the Forest itself.

At length they made up their minds to go on again. The path that had brought them to the hill reappeared on the northward side; but they had not followed it far before they became aware that it was bending steadily to the right. Soon it began to descend rapidly and they guessed that it must actually be heading towards the Withywindle valley: not at all the direction they wished to take. After some discussion they decided to leave this misleading path and strike northward; for although they had not been able to see it from the hill-top, the Road must lie that way, and it could not be many miles off. Also northward, and to the left of the path, the land seemed to be drier and more open, climbing up to slopes where the trees were thinner, and pines and firs replaced the oaks and ashes and other strange and nameless trees of the denser wood.

At first their choice seemed to be good: they got along at a fair speed, though whenever they got a glimpse of the sun in an open glade they seemed unaccountably to have veered eastwards. But after a time the trees began to close in again, just where they had appeared from a distance to be thinner and less tangled. Then deep folds in the ground were discovered unexpectedly, like the ruts of great giant-wheels or wide moats and sunken roads long disused and choked with brambles. These lay usually right across their line of march, and could only be crossed by scrambling down and out again, which was troublesome and difficult with their ponies. Each time they climbed down they found the hollow filled with thick bushes and matted undergrowth, which somehow would not yield to the left, but only gave way when they turned to the right; and they had to go some distance along the bottom before they could find a way up a further bank. Each time they clambered out, the trees seemed deeper and darker; and always to the left and upwards it was most difficult to find a way, and they were forced to the right and downwards.

After an hour or two they had lost all clear sense of direction, though they knew well enough that they had long ceased to go northward at all. They were being headed off, and were simply following a course chosen for them – eastwards and southwards, into the heart of the Forest and not out of it.

(from *The Lord of The Rings*, 1954)

Where the Bee Sucks, There Suck I

Where the bee sucks, there suck I,
In a cowslip's bell I lie;
There I couch when owls do cry.
On the bat's back I do fly
After summer merrily.
Merrily, merrily shall I live now,
Under the blossom that hangs on the bough.

(from *The Tempest*) WILLIAM SHAKESPEARE